Ruth

Ruth UNCENSORED

THE STORY YOU THOUGHT YOU KNEW

Jeff Ell

FURROW
PRESS

TO NEEN

CONTENTS

FOREWORD

T he book of Ruth has been a life-source for me personally. For such a short book, it packs a terrific punch. It's a powerful book that shows us a God who, above all else, is an extravagant Redeemer.

When you really understand this book, you shake your head at the fathomless Mercy, and give your heart away—again—to unconditional Acceptance and selfless Wealth.

Of the characters present in this colorful epic, you might (like me) identify most with the bitter heartsickness of Naomi. Or you might find yourself connecting more immediately with Ruth—the foreign widow—who somehow through the sorrows of life found a faith in the God of Israel that would not let go, even in the midst of grinding poverty.

How does God honor these two women who, despite a baptism of grief, preserve their consecration and cling to faith? The story concludes with Naomi holding in her arms the baby that lifts her reproach and establishes as her posterity the throne of David. And what about Ruth? The foreign widow becomes the desired bride, and through the fruit of her union with her redeemer-husband she becomes an ancestor to none other than Jesus Christ Himself.

But wait. If you think you've understood the message of the book of Ruth, the book you hold in your hands will make you think again. You're about to be surprised. My friend, Jeff Ell, is about to take you on a trek through the book of Ruth that will explore paths less trod. There are some turns ahead you never saw coming.

You'll find yourself thinking, "Did he just say that?" The honesty will startle you. Your cheeks may flush a bit. And your mind will churn—because this is a book that will make you think. And by the end, may you be left with renewed lovesickness for the glorious face of the Man who desired you enough to do whatever it took to bring you into His embrace.

Bob Sorge
Kansas City
August 2009

PREFACE

Ruth is the story of a young widow who slips under the blanket with a wealthy older man in the middle of the night. It's the story of a woman who arouses such passion in that man he marries her the next day. It's the rags to riches saga of a young widow's journey from impoverished alien to secure and beloved bride.

Ruth lays her body and soul at the feet of a man who could have exploited her vulnerability and availability. But what she got was the man's single-minded pursuit to secure her love and affection. She became his bride, and he bequeathed her with every temporal blessing he had, including his harvest.

Is there such a place today for the Bride of Christ at the feet of her Redeemer? Are there secret places and secret times in the night when we can ask our Redeemer to spread His covering over us? Is there a place of deeper intimacy where the Lover of our souls will pour the harvest into our cloaks? A place where we can stir His passion? Ruth, I believe, is a prophetic type of the Bride of Christ finding such a place at her Redeemer's feet.

Yes, I believe that such a place exists today—a place where His Bride can reap a harvest that she has not labored for, a place like Ruth found. A place where, in the cool shadows before the dawn, she receives the first fruits of the land she will soon own. A place where the back-breaking toil of manual labor underneath the equatorial sun gives way to a partnership of lovers, cultivating as one, the land He owns. A place where His embrace causes us to all but forget the aches and pains of the difficult labor He has asked us to join Him in.

This latter place is what Naomi, Ruth's mother-in-law, discovered. Hers had been a hard and painful journey, provoking her to refer to herself as Mara or bitter. Naomi returned to Israel as an emotionally wounded refugee. She buried hope in Moab along with her husband and two sons. The book of Ruth, therefore, is also a prophetic picture of the redemption of a weary and embittered generation as represented by Naomi. It shows us that, before Naomi died, she became the nurse to a grandson who joined the lineage of David and Christ. The blessing of Ruth reached into the prior generation and set it free from the bitterness and disappointment it had known.

I don't live in this place yet. My life and ministry seem to correspond much more closely to Ruth's days as a gleaner than as the Redeemer's Bride. I want to bear witness to His goodness to me. I've enjoyed His protection and provision. I've brought home the unusually bountiful harvest that can only be explained by His divine generosity. I love Him, He loves me, and I am more than happy to continue to pick up the sheaves He leaves for me to gather. But I am convinced there is much more.

Likewise, it seems like the people of God often have been relegated to the status of blessed gleaner rather than beloved Bride. We tend to gather just enough of the harvest to know that the Redeemer has noticed us. Yet rarely have we corporately entered into the fullness of His affections and provisions for us. This has been my experience anyway.

As you read this book, you will quickly discover that this is not a systematic exposition or comprehensive commentary on the book of Ruth. I'm sure there are any number of historical, grammatical and theological insights that others have more eloquently espoused. No, put simply, I'm merely interacting with the story—trying to see its relevancy for us today. It's my endeavor to glean, to garner what I can for my own journey and, if I may be so bold, for your journey, too.

Perhaps Ruth's book is most helpful to us all as a prophetic mirror. When we peer into its layered glass, we catch a glimpse of our Redeemer and ourselves—the double image of the Man God and the man. So don't be surprised when you discover our reflection is neither perfect nor complete. My life experience, like yours, has left some blemishes and scars—evidence of the perplexity, frustration and bitterness that are an inevitable part of the human condition. It would be good for us to stay focused on His image reflected in the life of Boaz, a redeemer whose life has given nearly three millennia of God's people an accurate image of our Redeemer's passion for us.

I also want to clearly state that I am not suggesting believers adopt some sort of reclusive or monastic lifestyle. So I ask that you not interpret these thoughts to be an endorsement of old-fashioned laziness cloaked in some quasi-spiritual existence. With more than six billion people on the earth today, this is not a time to be sleeping during the harvest. It's a time to partner with your Redeemer—to let Him free you from the bitterness and disappointment you have known. It's a time to get intimately acquainted with Him—to come to the personal place where He can pour the harvest into your cloak. It's my sincere prayer that you be blessed in your union with Him.

Jeff Ell
Roanoke
October 2009

CHAPTER 1
U-Hauls & Interstates

*"Now it came about . . . that there was a famine in the land.
And a certain man of Bethlehem in Judah went to sojourn in the land of Moab
with his wife and his two sons. And the name of the man was Elimelech,
and the name of his wife, Naomi; and the names of his two sons were
Mahlon and Chilion, Ephrathites of Bethlehem in Judah . . . . and the woman
was bereft of her two children and her husband"* (RUTH 1:1-5).

Hunger drove Elimelech out of the Promised Land. The land of plenty had turned into the land of not so much. It's sad and ironic that Bethlehem actually means house of bread. The name of their city must have taunted them each night they woke up while dreaming of food.

Starving people dream about food; sleep does not bring relief from the misery of hunger. The mental police that normally guard our minds in the night so we can sleep undisturbed are quickly overwhelmed by the rioting mobs of nerve endings demanding food. Pain is not long pacified or tricked back to sleep by the vivid hallucinations of gastronomic orgies projected on the jumbotrons on the back of eyelids. Pain receptors grow angry and shake their hungry owner awake in the middle of the night, demanding action.

Dreams and names were not feeding Elimelech's two boys; sips of water were not satisfying the nightly gnawing in their guts. They were starving, and someone needed to do something.

So Elimelech pulled up stakes, loaded up the U-haul and followed the interstate all the way to the border of Moab. Moab was a nation that bordered ancient Israel on the wrong side of the Dead Sea, a forbidden zone for the people of God. It was a place that practiced polytheism and didn't honor the One God of Abraham, Isaac and Jacob. It was a land ruled by pagans and governed by godlessness. It was a place the people of God were not supposed to visit and, most certainly, never meant to live. But Elimelech moved his family there anyway, out of the Promised Land and into Moab.

Maybe you've heard a sermon about Elimelech, the story of how he ran away from the Promised Land and dwelt in the sin of Moab. As a consequence of his faithless flight, no doubt you've heard the preacher say, "God punished him; he died and so did his two sons." Perhaps the preacher even paused, his eyes pleading with the congregation. And then, as he closed his eyes and slowly shook his head, he warned, "Brothers and sisters . . . don't be like old Elimelech!" Truth is it's a pretty easy sermon for stout preachers like me to preach after my Sunday morning three-egg omelet. But before I pass judgment on Elimelech, I must confess—I got some Elimelech in me.

Elimelech's flight to Moab is a prophetic picture of spiritually starving people. It's the story of a family without options, a family that was in so much pain it fled to the only place it thought it could find relief.

It's the untouched photos of people who got into real trouble and suffered real hurt. It's a prophetic glimpse of people who ran deeper into trouble while trying to run from it. It's the unedited, uncut version of two women who survived family tragedy and started their journey back home.

HUNGER POWER

Hunger moves us. Famine, gut-wrenching starvation and wasting malnutrition—the kind that stunts your baby's growth and arrests his mental development—will make all of us go places and eat things we never imagined. Naomi and her family knew this kind of hunger, and the names of her two sons tell us the story. Mahlon, meaning *sickly*, and Chilion, meaning *pining*, describe the physical state and health of sons born in a famine-stricken land. Their names told of their physical deprivation and need, but we can only imagine the heights or, more correctly, the depths Naomi and Elimelech went to give them relief.

People will eat almost anything to survive. The accounts of a rugby team stranded after an airplane crash in the mountains or a lost expedition that was attempting to discover the Northwest Passage are all pretty much the same. At first, they eat anything they can find: tooth paste, shoe leather and old animal skins all go down the hatch. Then the unimaginable happens; they start to eat . . . well, you know the story. Even when we are not actually starving, we will put all kinds of things in our mouths that are not very good for us. Just a few days of not eating enough will adjust our pallets and change our opinions about what's edible and what's not.

I'm reminded of the time two friends and I were on an extended road trip and had not eaten very much for a couple of days. We were short on cash and pretty hungry, so we decided to pick through the dumpster behind a bakery. After rummaging around for a couple of minutes, we found a flour sack full of both day-old doughnuts and garbage from the shop. Without thought or deliberation, we brushed off some of the coffee grinds and inhaled those doughnuts faster than Homer Simpson. Hunger lowered our inhibitions, and we ate those day-old delicacies without any concern or worry. That was many years ago, but I still remember where hunger plunged me.

I've never experienced *real* famine or starvation, though. I live in America, a place of such natural abundance that the poor are often overweight. The hunger that drives me out of the Promised Land is spiritual and soulish in nature. The enemy's advertisements and solicitations kindle illegitimate hunger pangs that smolder in my soul. They start fires of discontentment that burn hotter the more I try to douse their flames with the very things they make me burn for—the same way those glamour shots of juicy burgers elicit illicit hunger pangs that keep the drive-thru busy till closing time. This hunger is not authentic, but the discomfort is enough to get me to eat things that are unable to satisfy my real craving. I find myself snacking on junk food imported directly from Egypt. (I especially like the barbecue flavored leeks and onions.)

Sin, immoral thoughts and behaviors promise a quick solution to the pain in our souls. I'm fascinated and mesmerized by the diversity of sin which is so readily available to any consumer of evil shopping in the world today. Yesterday's mom and pop little sin shops have been replaced by giant supercenters that sell everything our corrupted natures could ever want. It's as if the black-and-white world of the previous generation has instantly gone color—like that moment when Dorothy wakes up in Oz, oh my, the colors, the sights, the smells. The black-and-white world of my evangelical Kansas has been swallowed up by the Technicolor, HiDef hues of a demonically-colored Moab. I must get up and escape this godless land.

This soul hunger is also a lot like the hunger I feel a few hours after eating Thanksgiving dinner. On that glorious Thursday when our culture pronounces absolution over the sin of gluttony, I cram enough calories into me for a week. More stuffing, more potatoes, more dark meat . . . more of everything, thank you very much! My appetite is the quintessential spoiled brat—no matter how much junk I stuff in its mouth, it never shuts up.

Genuine spiritual hunger, on the other hand, motivates me to seek a deeper relationship with the Lord. I become like the people of Israel when they were hungry for meat, as they *craved intensely in the wilderness, and tempted God in the desert. So He gave them their request, but sent a wasting disease among them*" (Ps. 106:14-15).

This famine of the soul and spirit starts me on my journey back to Him. I become the famished prodigal who comes to his senses and starts back to the family farm.

The cotton candy of our materialistic society, the lack of spiritual authority, the impotence of the Christian community—all leave me craving for *real* spiritual food. The tasteless, low-cal, fat-free, white-bread messages that are passed over the counters of the cloned-franchised faith outlets are not meeting my spirit's nutritional needs. I need to eat the true Bread, the unprocessed whole grain Manna of the Body of Christ Himself.

This Spirit-induced hunger motivates me to leave the Moabs I have felt compelled to seek refuge in. These legitimate hunger pangs drive my skinny soul from the La-Z-Boy lifestyle that has ensconced my emaciated spirit for far too long. Unfortunately, this starvation diet has also weakened me so much that leaving becomes increasingly difficult.

Sometimes, I have felt like a spiritual skeleton—no fat, no muscle and no energy to escape the famine—the spiritual equivalent of the emaciated inmates of concentration camps who were too feeble to walk out of the prisons they dreamed of escaping from for so long. Starvation had left the survivors of the holocaust too weak to appropriate their emancipation. Maybe you've seen the black-and-white movies of those poor souls who just stared in disbelief at the Allied troops who had come to set them free. Like them, I stare at the Cross but can't walk in the freedom it brings. I hear the words announcing my emancipation from Satan's slavery but am just too weak to walk away. How alike I am to the emaciated prisoners who needed to be slowly fed and nursed to health before they could stand and walk out of prison on their own. I'm so grateful for my Redeemer's loving care, for the times when He has fed me when I could not feed myself.

RELOCATIONS

Our family moved after almost 20 years in one place. It was a good move, a God-ordained and God-blessed relocation. Maybe you've recently relocated or remarried, or started a new job in a new place. I hope things are going as well for you as they have gone for us. Or maybe today you're alone in a foreign land, a long way from home; maybe you've thought about returning home. I hope you'll start back today. Maybe you're too weak to walk; I trust you'll experience your Redeemer's gentle feeding of your soul with small bits of spiritual bread. Not too much too quickly, remember starving people can only eat little bits of food at first.

Of course, not all relocations are well-conceived; not all sojourning is at the leading of the Lord. Often the promise of a new and prosperous life turns out to be the sad unpacking of the same old problems in a new locale. A change in address will never address an issue of the heart. Unresolved issues will turn fresh green grass a familiar brown overnight.

The idea of starting over in a new place can be a very powerful temptation, especially if the move is meant to avoid the discomfort of addressing the core issues causing pain in our souls and lives. The temporary relief offered by relocation, re-churching and re-marriage are especially appealing when we know or suspect that re-solving core issues will be costly and painful.

Elimelech and Naomi's move to Moab seems to have been like this. The two boys were wedded, thus leading us to believe that there may have been a season of relative prosperity for this troubled family. I'm sure Naomi must have wished for a grandson after her boys got married. Like all want-to-be-grandmothers, she would have furtively scanned Orpah's and Ruth's bellies from time to time, looking for some swelling evidence of new life. The birth of a grandchild would surely usher in better days and right their battered family ship. *Maybe things will work out after all*, she could have thought to herself. The move, the new nation, her sons now married—perhaps it started to look like a real solution. But then the ship sank.

UNCENSORED TESTIMONIES

The text just states the facts, *"The woman was bereft of her two children and her husband"* (Ruth 1:5). The Scriptures don't use adjectives to describe her pain. It would be like describing the Grand Canyon as *big* or flowers in the rainforest as *beautiful*. Bottle rockets have a better chance at reaching the moon than words have of describing what life must have been like for Naomi.

Their move to Moab may have been unavoidable; maybe Naomi was opposed to it from the start; maybe it was her idea. We will never know. What we do know is that whatever pain and suffering she experienced back in Israel was dwarfed by what she was going through now. Things go from bad to worse, and her life's story reads like a Russian novel. Her nuclear family is buried while she is living in exile. It's the opening line in every story of redemption. And we readers get to learn vicariously through the uncensored testimony of the narrative.

That's why it's not just okay to tell our stories like the Bible tells Naomi's and Ruth's—it's essential! I want to suggest that we would do well to follow the court's instructions to witnesses, that we would "tell the whole truth and nothing but the truth." Our cleaned-up narratives entice travelers to begin their journeys but do little to prepare them for the inevitable hardships and stark realities of what it really takes to make it home.

Too often, our teaching lacks power because our stories have been filtered through the cheesecloth of religious culture. We end up with a soupy predictability so lacking in spiritual nutrition that anyone subsisting on its watery broth becomes too weak to escape our religious gulags.

Redemption is a story of hanging in public, without a loin cloth. It's the family album full of gory pictures of torture and ignoble death. It's the account of real people in real hell holes, stories where everyone you love dies. The Scriptures don't edit the less palatable parts of its heroes' and heroines' stories. The chunky facts are not puréed by well-meaning religious editors who want to make the Christian life easier to swallow.

How is it then we are still surprised by the spiritual sickness that has the Body of Christ bedridden in our spiritual Moabs? Why do we continue to hustle the snake oil of perpetual health and un-spendable wealth to a diseased constituency that languishes in the nursing homes of our insipid religion? Our cathedrals have been converted into long-term nursing facilities from which no one ever leaves. We tilt heads and spoon-feed drops of useless platitudes into the mouths of a dying generation. We have become the practitioners of palliative medicine. Our messages are laced with the opiates of false faith that dulls the pain and helps the dying sleep.

We play bingo and hire clergy to staff our spiritual hospices. Generations slip away in a painless fog while well-spoken people with bleached teeth tell them everything is going to be fine. If we are going to recover, we will first need a dose of the truth—the kind of truth my friend Joe told to an accident victim.

Joe is an EMT. One afternoon, he and his brother were out driving on some back roads when a call came through on his scanner. A young man had fallen down a ravine, and a farmer had called 911 when he heard the man's screams for help. They happened to be near the accident scene, so he and his brother were the first ones to scramble down the steep cliffs to where the young man lay in a twisted heap. His femur bone was sticking out of his thigh, bloody white bone protruded through his wool hunting pants. Joe's brother looked away to keep from getting sick.

A little later reinforcements appeared on the rim of the cataract. A couple of the braver volunteer firemen and rescue squad members made their way down the cliffs while the rest lowered a caged stretcher with a rope. After stabilizing the patient and sliding him into the emergency gurney, they awaited the signal to begin man-hauling him up the steep bank. Before they did, Joe took a firm hold of the rope and looked the victim in the eye. He said, "This is going to hurt worse than anything you've ever experienced." He let go of the rope and waved up at the crew. The rope grew taut as the excruciating assent began. The kid screamed and moaned all the way up.

Maybe you feel like you're at the bottom of a ravine. Maybe you're in the Moab of your own choices. Maybe your life, your soul is all twisted and broken. Before we go any further in the story, I want to look you in the eye and tell you that getting to safety will probably hurt worse than anything else you've ever experienced. Getting out of hell hurts like hell, so go ahead and scream all you want. I sure have.

CHAPTER 2
Married Before

*"And they took for themselves Moabite women as wives;
the name of the one was Orpah and the name of the other Ruth"* (RUTH 1:4).

*"'All that you have done for your mother-in-law after the death of your husband
has been fully reported to me . . .'"* (RUTH 2:11).

Ruth was not a virgin. She was a widow. She had been married to Chilion, Naomi and Elimelech's youngest son. That union did not produce any surviving children, and that's all we know about their marriage. Yet Boaz knew this about Ruth and was not dissuaded from his desire to marry her. Because Chilion was dead, her second marriage to Boaz was completely legitimate and legal. However, this did not change the fact that she had known another man.

All of humanity is like Ruth; no one comes to the Redeemer as a virgin. We've all had other lovers of some kind. No one can flaunt her perfection or her virtue in front of the Lord and think the Lord will be wowed by her holiness. I don't think I've ever met someone who honestly thought his holiness qualified him to be with God. A more common experience is the feeling that we've done things that have disqualified us from getting married to the Redeemer.

It's easy to believe that our sordid and jaded pasts—with all the depravation, guilt and shame—have made us undesirable to Him. At the very least, we may think we deserve to be relegated to some sort of second-class existence because of our pasts. We see ourselves as damaged goods that need to be kept off the dance floor.

Ruth is a prophetic image of the Body of Christ—a Body comprised of imperfect people with less-than-perfect personal histories. I hear the voice of the Spirit speaking through these passages. He is reminding us that there is no place we've been, and no one we've been with, that could ever make us ineligible for marriage to Him. He is silencing the persuasive lies of the enemy, the lies that tell us we're too ugly, too fat and too diseased for a rich Redeemer to even notice us, let alone want to marry us. Our enemy gossips about us. He employs legions of angry reporters who attempt to soil our reputations and dislodge us from our relationship with our Redeemer.

HELL'S PAPARAZZI

Paparazzi is the familiar name given to people who photograph celebrities and sell the images to the press. The expression is Italian and is thought to come from the nicknaming of a particularly noisy mosquito that was after an infamously busy photographer portrayed in an old movie. A pesky mosquito is a good way to describe these hyperactive photographers who are in orbit around their famous prey.

At public events, armies of paparazzi line up and shoot volleys of pictures into the ranks of the rich and famous as they march into premiers and award shows. (Maybe all that shooting is why the carpet is red.) These are photo ops that celebrities are ready for. They play to the cameras, flashing their smiles and twirling in their designer clothes.

But what the paparazzi are famous for and what they really want are opportunities to photograph celebrities in private moments, or even better, embarrassing situations. To get these images, the paparazzi will do just about anything. They become camouflaged snipers with telescopic lenses crouching in the jungle near a tropical beach. They hang out of low flying helicopters that buzz private weddings. They spare no expense in their efforts because cheesy tabloids pay big money for the right to publish those images.

Maybe you never realized that every follower of Christ is a celebrity. We are famous, not because we're rich or glamorous; we're famous because we are engaged to the King of the universe, because we are destined to walk down the aisle with the most important Man in history. Everything we do and say has now become news. Whether we realize it or not, hell's paparazzi are shooting us from every angle and at every opportunity to catch us in unflattering poses. They are trying to get the dirt on us.

The mastermind of hell's paparazzi is Satan himself, the accuser of the brethren, who the Bible says, *"accuses us before our God day and night"* (Rev. 12:10). He keeps track of where we've been, what we've done and what we've said. Every transgression or infraction is photographed by the demonic paparazzi that buzz about the believer's life.

Hell's tabloids report the gossip and print the images that are published in heaven in a futile attempt to get God to disown us. The attempt is futile because our Redeemer has already made a solemn covenant to return and marry His Bride. He knows who we are and where we've been, and none of that has kept Him from loving us.

Nonetheless, and in spite of the ultimate futility of it, 24 hours a day the accuser of the brethren gossips about the Bride of Christ. He starts rumors, embellishes facts and does whatever he can to make her look ugly and portray her as a whore.

When Jesus returns, He will do so as the Lion, His eyes will be filled with holy rage, and there will be no mercy on that day for those who have slandered His Bride. There are few things that will stir anger in a man more than someone speaking trash about his wife. When our Bridegroom returns, He will break the accuser's filthy jaw and shatter his lying teeth! He does not take kindly to people talking poorly about His woman.

As the wedding day draws closer, it seems as if the enemy is working frantically to do as much damage to the Bride as he can in his limited time. Maybe he is thinking if he can defile her, scar her and shame her enough, the Bridegroom will find her so repugnant that He will not follow through with the wedding.

Satan is doing everything he can to make the Church look more like a cheap hooker than a radiant young Bride. As the end of this age draws to a close, it seems as though Satan is working overtime to do as much damage as he can to the Bride while he still has the chance.

Sleeping with another man's wife is a serious subject. It is probably the ultimate revenge, the worst kind of retribution that could be meted out to an enemy. Satan wants to get to the Bride before Jesus does. He wants to molest her, grope her and seduce her. He wants to broadcast to the world that he has been doing it with Jesus' fiancée.

The seduction of the Bride is Satan's ministry. Every Christian is part of the Bride of Christ; therefore, each of us has been propositioned; each of us has been hit on by the Savior's archenemy. It's our privilege to turn, give the enemy the cold shoulder and glory in the promise of Christ's return.

FULL DISCLOSURE

The broadcasting of our embarrassing moments by Satan is futile for a second reason. The reason is that we have already told the Father everything, so everything has been forgiven and forgotten. Full disclosure to the Father removes any leverage the enemy has in his accusations. If he starts talking about us by saying, "Did you know that on last Tuesday at precisely 10:07 p.m. the accused, your so-called child, did this?" He slides the photos across the desk or replays the video. Our Father simply responds, "As a matter of fact, I do. He told me all about it just before you got here."

Funny how politicians have discovered the power of this Biblical principle. Have you noticed recently that more and more people running for public office seem to kick off their candidacy by disclosing any immoral or questionable events from their pasts? They volunteer information about how they smoked pot or belonged to a fringe political action committee. They have figured out that introducing their skeletons in a press conference is preferable to having them jump out of the closet a couple of days before the election

If you have received Christ as Lord and Savior, you are a child of God, and nothing can change that reality. However, these images of our failures can make us doubt the reality of our relationship with Him. Our sin, mistakes and indiscretions cause us to shrink back from His holy presence. Embarrassed children of God are often tempted to run away and hide from their Father.

But we can access His cleansing by continually judging ourselves rightly and confessing our sins honestly and immediately. Personal responsibility is the very thing that allows us to escape the condemnation coming upon the world (1 Cor. 11:32).

The enemy hates this; he hates confession. When we confess, he has nothing to use against us. This is why he always tries to convince us to get involved in some kind of cover up. He tries to persuade us not to confess our sins to God or to one another. He misrepresents our Father's and our friends' responses to our sin. He does this to keep us away from the bathtub.

Thankfully, the mud and grime caked on our bodies do nothing to change the fact that we are God's children. He can certainly use a stiff brush and harsh soap if that's what it takes to clean us up, but we are still His kids in Christ. Bath time is private family time, so only our loving Father can bathe us, cleanse us and sanctify us. Only the Husband of the Bride, Jesus Christ is authorized to bathe her. As Paul writes: *"That He might sanctify her, having cleansed her by the washing of the water with the Word, that He might present to Himself the church in all her glory, having no spot or wrinkle or any such thing; but that she should be holy and blameless"* (Eph. 5:26-27).

God is good and knows what is best for us, so only He determines our discipline. Only he knows what best teaches and trains us to walk in right-eousness. Each child is different; some need only a word while others need something more stringent. The enemy does not get to decide how to disci-pline us. The Father is working by His Spirit to mature us into the image of His Son. The enemy would simply use the opportunity to torture us, humil-iate us, embitter us and slowly kill us. There is nothing redemptive, nothing cleansing or reviving in Satan's plan of pain. Part of his strategy is to convince us that we are no longer welcome in the Father's presence.

Christian ministry is supposed to be the exact opposite of Satan's. This is why Paul describes his ministry in 2 Corinthians 11:2 this way: *"For I am jealous for you with a godly jealousy; for I betrothed you to one husband, that to Christ I might present you as a pure virgin."* Ministry is the supernatural work of the Spirit of God whereby non-virgins are miraculously transformed into virgins. The corruption of sin is undone by the grace of God, and our past and future are perfectly and flawlessly redeemed.

That's why it's good to be careful about what we say and how we say it. It's so easy to criticize the Church, especially when she is not looking her best after a long week in the sun. It's somewhat paradoxical that we would never tell an engaged or a married woman she needs to lose weight, or that she is lazy, or that her teeth are crooked and her acne looks like it's getting worse. Yet, it's all too common for folks publically addressing a body of believers to do just that—berating them for their ugliness and shortcomings in mean-spirited harangues. No wonder so many believers look so sad!

We're constantly being reminded how un-virtuous and ugly we are by the accusations of the enemy, so we need more finger-pointing from our family, right? In no way am I suggesting that sermons and teachings become the syrupy motivational chats that seem to have become very popular in our western church culture. Our messages must come from the Bible, and the Word of God is meant for teaching, reproof, correction and training in righteousness (2 Tim. 3:16).

All I'm saying is we should remember that Jesus is madly in love with the Church, and we would do well to be mindful of that when we are given the privilege of talking to her.

It is difficult to grasp His attraction to us. What does He see in me individually, and what does He see in us corporately that is so appealing? Nevertheless, He is crazy about us, and He is returning to marry us.

HE MARRIED WHOM?

Not only was Ruth not a virgin, she also was not the most fashionable young woman in Bethlehem. If you don't have enough money for food, it's unlikely you're wearing Prada and sporting Cartier.

A day laboring in the sun is not like a day at the spa, sipping fruity drinks with cucumbers on your eyes. Tanned skin was a mark of poverty; it was irrefutable evidence of one's social standing. It would have been impossible for Ruth to disguise her humble status. Perhaps Ruth felt like Solomon's beloved who said, *"'Do not stare at me because I am swarthy, for the sun has burned me'"* (Song of Sol. 1:6). Let's face it—Ruth was a very unlikely object of her redeemer's affections. She was a real-life Cinderella. She was the "I never saw that one coming" selection of a man who could have had any single woman he wanted.

My suspicion is that after the wedding most of the locals were wagging their heads, thinking and whispering that Boaz could have done a lot better than Ruth. The beguiling blessing of the elders spoken over Boaz subtly conveys the community's less-than-wholehearted support or understanding of this union. Certainly, there would have been any number of cute local girls who would have been thrilled to have Boaz come courting—virgins from good families.

I'm sure Boaz was often invited over for dinner to meet the well-kept young women whose dads were respected in the city, girls whose pedigrees and social status were more fitting for someone of Boaz's position and stature, and more specifically, girls who were Jewish!

If I put my ear up to the text, I can almost hear the good folks of Bethlehem remarking to one another in hushed tones over their lattes . . .

"I don't know what he sees in her."

"I heard the little thing just threw herself at him."

"I say she's already pregnant, and they had to get married."

"We should lift them up at prayer meeting tonight."

We don't know if Obed was a honeymoon baby; if he was, I'll guarantee more than one person in Bethlehem was doing some mental arithmetic when they met Naomi standing in the checkout line at the market. When I put my ear back up against my Bible, I think I can hear a conversation that went something like this:

"Hi, Naomi. Good to see you. How's that new grandson of yours?"

"Oh, wonderful. Let me show you some pictures. I just got these developed at the pharmacy." (Neighbor smiles as Naomi unfurls dozens of pictures. She politely glances at them.)

"And how are the proud parents?"

"Oh, they're doing just great. Boaz is so good with that baby!"

"Now, tell me again, when did those two get married?"

"Right after the wheat harvest."

"How nice. Such a lovely time for a wedding. Was it a large service?"

"No, just a few family and close friends."

"How nice . . . and tell me again. How old is the baby now?"

"Just a month old."

(Pregnant pause in the conversation. The neighbor's eyes move left to right several times.)

"Oh, praise the Lord! You must be very proud. See you later."

"Bye, stop in anytime. I have more pictures . . . ."

A friend told me that a pregnant pause is the amount of time it takes to figure in your brain if someone got pregnant before they got married. Did you know that religious people have the ability to do math while keeping sympathetic-looking smiles pasted on their faces? In their heads, they're counting seven, eight, nine, ten . . . then out loud they blurt, "Oh, praise the Lord!" Later, when they get back home, they get out the calendar and check to make sure they crunched the numbers properly in their head. Wouldn't it be nice to be part of a community where no one was counting or keeping score, a farsighted community in which older brothers and sisters regularly look out upon the horizon for a familiar silhouette?

But let's get back to the redeeming character in the story. Boaz was a very eligible bachelor, as we mentioned earlier. We are told that he was *"a man of great wealth"* (Ruth 2:1). Wealthy men tend to marry attractive women because women find money very attractive. Now let's not act too religiously. We all have seen some normal-looking guy with a stunning wife and thought, "He must be rich." We don't have any photos of Ruth; we don't know what she looked like. But we are certain of this—she was poor and worked in the fields and that made it impossible for her to look her best. Nonetheless, Boaz falls for this poor, dusty, sweaty, foreign girl.

This is a beautiful and accurate picture of Christ's love for us individually and His love for the Church corporately. He didn't come into the world to save only virgins or beautiful people. His love for mankind encompasses everyone (Titus 3:4). He is head-over-heels in love with folks that are not the most attractive or most eligible by human standards. *"God sees not as man sees, for man looks at the outward appearance, but the Lord looks at the heart"* (1 Sam. 16:7).

You don't have to be a movie star or win a beauty contest to garner His attention. I try to remember this when I'm around His people. I try to remember He is engaged to the Church. I try to remember this even when I look in the mirror.

It does not matter that Ruth was married before—not to her redeemer. And it means nothing to our Redeemer. He, like Boaz, does not notice the other young maidens. It does not matter that we just got off the road from Moab; He is not focused on our worn-out clothes and tattered sandals. He sees past the sweat streaking our dusty faces. He ignores our sun-baked skin and gazes into our eyes. He has set His love upon us. And we, like Ruth, will soon be emancipated by our marriage to the Redeemer.

CHAPTER 3
Orpah

"And they lifted up their voices and wept again; and Orpah kissed her mother-in-law, but Ruth clung to her. Then she said, 'Behold, your sister-in-law has gone back to her people and her gods . . .'" (RUTH 1:14-15).

O rpah never made it out of Moab. For a number of apparently logical reasons, she separated from Naomi and returned to Moab. She returned to the safety and familiarity of her native land and walked off the pages of Scripture.

Orpah is a negative prophetic archetype of those who remain bound to their old lives and old lands in spite of having been given the opportunity to leave. She is a prophetic picture of those who remain lost in the carnal and natural world and never enter into the destiny where intimacy with the Redeemer leads them. Personally, I find it much more enjoyable to be led by positive role models, but we have agreed to tell the whole story, and I think we can learn something from her mistakes.

First, let's reaffirm that becoming disoriented from time to time is part of every believer's journey. No one gets it right every time. Old Testament heroes like Abraham strayed into Egypt, and King David got turned around with Bathsheba. Even New Testament apostles like Peter became directionally challenged more than once during their exemplary lives. Take, for example, when Peter conveniently forgot whom he was following in Caiaphas's courtyard and denied knowing Jesus three times (Luke 22:60-62). He got lost a second time, a number of years later, when he was under the influence of the legalists in Galatia. Peter was disoriented by pseudo-Christians who were trying to hide the path of grace with the debris of religion so gentiles would not find the Lord. Peter didn't know where he was until Paul came and set him on the right path (Gal. 1:11-14). These are just a couple of examples of God's people who got offtrack.

The real issue, of course, is not our getting directionally challenged from time to time. Orpah helps us see that the real issue is whether or not we will stay disoriented. Thomas's confession of "Lord, we don't know where You are going? How do we know the way?" resonates in every follower of Jesus. Christ's response of "I'm the way" glistens like the polar star on a cold cloudless night. If you're lost, go throw your arms around Him. He will guide you on the path that all humanity is meant to walk. Call out to a trusted friend who can help you get reoriented.

Sadly, Orpah's response vicariously teaches us what not to do. Learning from her mistakes and the mistakes of others hopefully will spare us, our families and friends of much heartache, grief and wasted time.

In the next chapter, I would like to share a more positive and Biblical pattern of being guided and making decisions that Ruth exemplifies. But before we ride along with Naomi and Ruth on their journey to Bethlehem, let's take a look at some of the typical detours we can find ourselves in.

TEARS

Orpah, you'll remember, cried just as much as Ruth did, yet still ended up staying in Moab. If we look closely enough, we can see some qualities in Orpah that are typical of overly sentimental and maudlin religion that is unable to carry its devotees to the Promised Land.

In spite of the intensity of the experience—the whirling dervishes and the tear-soaked altars—we discover this brand of religion is just a narrow-gauged track that goes in a circle. After being dropped off at the same exact spot a few hundred Monday mornings in a row, it eventually dawns on us we've been on an emotional roller coaster in an amusement park that just happens to have a religious theme. Sometimes, we even scream and raise our hands on the steepest and fastest section of track to heighten the experience. Then, we engage in the ritualized tearful break-up between feelings and action. Orpah cried as she made the U-turn back to Moab.

Emotionalism and tears in some religious gatherings become the authentication of sincerity, a currency we mistakenly believe buys life-changing mercy and grace. But not all tears are the same.

Scientists have discovered that the chemical composition of tears changes, depending on why they are shed. Our eyes produce tears when we are grieving that have traces of the enzymes and hormones released in our brains during times of stress and mental pain. Apparently, tears are the body's way of venting and then flushing away the build-up of these powerful chemicals. The release of this pressure is undoubtedly part of the reason why having a good cry actually feels good.

The tears our eyes produce when irritated by allergies, a sharp stick or dry air are free from these chemicals. While they come from the same place and are necessary to wash away irritants and lubricate our dry eyes, they are not the same.

Here is the point—both Ruth and Orpah cried, but only Ruth turned her tear-stained face toward her future destiny in the land of Judah. Orpah's tears floated her back around to Moab. Hers were the same kind of tears we shed to wash away the irritants of sin or the sharp stick of conviction. It's the emotional credit card accepted by religions everywhere—religions that have fashioned flexible Jesus action figures fitting neatly into their own culture's pocket; the NASCAR, Left Turn Only Jesus, who swoops into car wrecks and hospital rooms at the last second and fends off the Grim Reaper in the nick of time; the Wedding Jesus, Christmas Jesus, Funeral Jesus, Cry When I Get Caught Jesus and Walk In A Circle Jesus—every Jesus other than the Lord Jesus who has come to take me out of my Moab.

FEAR

Naomi paints a realistic picture of what life in the Promised Land will be like for her daughters-in-law. Three times, she tells them to return to Moab, that life in Bethlehem holds little promise of being good or easy (Ruth 1:8, 11-12). Three times, she reminds them that, in all likelihood, they are going to be widows just like her for the rest of their lives. Nonetheless, it was still a mistake for Orpah to be guided by her fears of what life would be like in Bethlehem. Similarly, it is a mistake for us to make decisions because of our fear of what might happen to us or our families in the future.

There are more than 200 official phobias recognized by the American

Psychological Association—arachnophobia, claustrophobia, xenophobia, this, that and the other phobia. My suspicion is that the list of debilitating fears plaguing humanity will continue to lengthen as we move ever closer to the end of this age. As darkness increases, the bondage that fear brings will be on the increase, especially the fear of death and dying (Heb. 2:14-15).

God's people, however, are not meant to be guided by fear. Fear-based decisions are rarely healthy decisions. Fear-based decisions tend to shrink our world into an ever smaller safety zone. We bubble-wrap our lives until we are suffocated by the very things we thought would insulate us from the risks and challenges we were created to face with the Lord. We are emotional hostages handcuffed and sequestered from the faith-based existence He has invited us to share with Him.

I feel for Orpah. On that day, she turned around and walked off the pages of Scripture. She had no idea she might be giving up the opportunity to bless every generation that would come after her with a testimony similar to Ruth's. Who knows? Maybe today we would find the book of Ruth and Orpah right between Judges and 1 Samuel.

Let's learn from Orpah's life—let's learn how not to be led by fear, how not to allow fear to detour us from the Lord's leading and direction. I've discovered other potential detours in life that seem pertinent to this discussion about mistakes we can make while seeking the leading and guidance of the Lord.

CIRCUMSTANCES

A completely unreliable determiner of direction is the wind of circumstance. Circumstances blow from every direction, and our carnal nature has a conflicting and base interest promoting *comfort* and *convenience* as the final arbiters of God's will. We lick our manicured fingers and stick them into the wind so we can set a course that follows the path of least resistance. We test the waters of public opinion and chart a new course only when the barometer of consensus lets us know that there will be smooth sailing ahead. Our private yachts stay safely moored in wave-less harbors, gently bobbing in the low risk waters of convention and status quo.

It's pretty safe to assume circumstance played a major role in leading

Orpah back to the comfort and convenience of Moab. Following Ruth back to Israel was going to be anything but comfortable and convenient. Storm flags were flying at that place in the road where Orpah and Naomi parted company. It was an overland journey, but Naomi made it clear some rough seas lay ahead.

There were the typical depravations associated with a long foot march—hunger, thirst and threat of assault along the way. Once they reached their destination, the inevitable pain of adjusting to life in a foreign land awaited her. Moving into the Promised Land meant being separated from every familiar comfort of Moab.

I confess I'm like Orpah sometimes. If we were honest, I think all of us can understand her decision to stay home. Like her, we put Kingdom business on our calendars when it's convenient. We head in the opposite direction whenever something, someplace or someone makes us feel uncomfortable.

All of us understand the desire to stay in the leeward side of conflict, confrontation and risk. Comfortable situations and convenient circumstances become the only destinations we mistakenly believe God has called us to live in. This principle has value in so many of the situations we find ourselves in here in this age and culture.

Just because the bank accepted our loan application does not mean Jesus is leading us into debt. The fact that the plasma TV I've always wanted went on sale the same day I went to Best Buy to look at it doesn't necessarily mean that God "definitely wanted me to have it." Discovering the church across town has pony rides and childcare from the moment we enter it till the moment we leave does not necessarily mean we're "being led to attend there." Realizing that my bank account is pretty low should not be interpreted as God's personal revelation that He doesn't want me to give. I've gotten blown off course whenever I've attempted to navigate using the winds of circumstance as my guide.

Let's learn from Orpah's life—let's look at two other potential detours in life that seem pertinent to any discussion about making life-changing decisions. These are two things that we have no evidence distracted Orpah, but these can certainly distract us.

IMPERSONATION

This consistently uphill journey of following and clinging to Christ can seem almost impossible for those of us who see ourselves as just average believers. I know some profoundly spiritual people who seem to live at a different altitude than I can survive at, and climb at a pace I can't maintain. Like those rare individuals who have conquered Mount Everest without bottled oxygen, these unusually gifted individuals seem to be always climbing, able to pray without ceasing, fast without headaches and do the work of the ministry 70 hours a week for decades without ever waning in strength or fervor. They become the featured speakers at our conferences and write the books that set the standards we're all supposed to follow. Supermoms and superpastors, their smiling faces are on the covers of parenting magazines and how-to-do ministry books. They map out strategies that are guaranteed to lead us to the Promised Land of success. Along the way, I have discovered I am not that kind of person.

All of us tend to idolize superstars, both natural athletes and these elite spiritual athletes. As children, we try to mimic the moves and styles of our favorite team's best players. We play imaginary games by ourselves in the driveway. We hear the announcer's voice in our brains, "Eleven seconds left on the clock. He dribbles behind his back, escapes the double-team, gets both feet behind the three-point line. Two seconds. He spins. One second. He shoots . . . he misses." We reset the clock and try again. Imitating superstars definitely does not endow us with their talents.

A few years ago, I got on my daughter Gwen's skateboard and tried to do a jump just like I had seen her and her friends do. To be completely honest, my attempt was actually more of a hop than a jump. (Up till now, you were thinking I was kind of smart.) Anyway, this attempted hop ended the only way it could have. It ended with a well-nourished 45-year-old man writhing on the driveway in agony, with his wife shaking her head in the kitchen window. No trip to the emergency room that time, and there will be no next time. I've come to realize I can't successfully impersonate superstars or anyone else, for that matter, without getting hurt.

Both in the natural world and the spiritual world, there is this tendency to mimic the moves and abilities of uniquely gifted individuals. Emergency rooms are kept busy setting the broken bones of kids who were trying to skate like Tony Hawk. They are full of middle-aged men with wrist problems caused by trying to hit the ball out of the rough on Saturday morning like Tiger does on Sunday afternoon.

Churches are full of broken people who got hurt trying to become the next spiritual superstar by aping the perceived lifestyle of a spiritual athlete with a unique calling and gifting. Entire congregations are broken because of their failed attempt to import and imitate the methods that worked for another congregation.

It is essential that we learn from those who have gone before us as well as those who have insights and observations that will improve our lives. But we will hurt ourselves and those around us if we simply attempt to imitate those gifted few who do all things well.

PROPHECY

An unreliable determiner of direction is prophecy. If you're of the opinion that prophecy is for today, don't slam this book shut just yet because I am of the same opinion. And if you're of the opinion that prophecy was only a first-century phenomenon, don't get too excited and raise your hands in agreement with this statement just yet either. Let me explain.

God inspires the minds and mouths of humans to speak forth His Word and will. A sermon delivered from a passage of Scripture at just the right moment is prophetic by definition. The Spirit is highlighting a specific truth at just the right moment for the benefit of the person listening to the sermon or teaching. It's why a believer will approach the pastor of even the most conservative church and say, "Pastor, that word was just for me." God uses people to bring attention to specific aspects of His revelation for the benefit of His people.

Additionally, a believer can possess the gift of prophecy today. It is a spiritual gift that enables one to hear and understand specifics about the lives and circumstances of people around them. The prophet is then able to articulate this God-given information so as to bring *"edification and exhortation and consolation"* (1 Cor.14:3). I am so grateful for the accurate words spoken to me by people with this wonderful gift. But personalized prophetic words are not meant to be used as a stand-alone formula for determining the directions of our lives.

Prophecy is, at its very best, a partial revelation of God's will. That's why Paul wrote, *"For we know in part, and we prophesy in part"* (1 Cor. 13:9). It is a mistake to set our courses based solely on these partial revelations because it eliminates the most important part of being led, that of intimacy with Him.

The rightful place of prophecy is to confirm that we are still on the right path, to strengthen us to continue on our way even when the journey is difficult and to warn us of trouble that may await us on our God-given path. Here is a Biblical example that illustrates this truth.

Acts 21:10-11 says, *". . . a certain prophet named Agabus came down from Judea. And coming to us, he took Paul's belt and bound his own feet and hands, and said, 'This is what the Holy Spirit says: "In this way the Jews in Jerusalem will bind the man who owns this belt and deliver him into the hands of the Gentiles."'"* Note that Paul was already on his way to Jerusalem when Agabus the prophet prophesied to him. Agabus performs a mini-prophetic skit and then tells him about the dangers that were ahead, a word that must have brought great comfort to Paul after his arrest and imprisonment.

As we can see by this example, prophecies are meant to serve like road signs on dark country roads. They awaken new strength when we are tired and feel like we can't go any further. They exhort us to pay attention to the dangerous curves ahead. They bring us consolation and comfort when we're convinced we must have taken a wrong turn at that intersection many miles back. But in spite of its many wonderful benefits, prophecy was never meant to be a substitute for finding direction that flows from intimacy with Him. Intimacy, we will discover, is the way Ruth got to Bethlehem.

CHAPTER 4
Bi-directional Orientation

". . . but Ruth clung to her . . . . 'Do not urge me to leave you or turn back from following you; for where you go, I will go, and where you lodge, I will lodge. Your people shall be my people, and your God, my God'" (RUTH 1:14-16).

Making decisions is rarely easy. Just think about the time you were in a car with three or four others trying to decide on where to go for lunch. Chances are, you quickly learned even a trivial decision like that can turn into a mini riot. Or what about the time you went into a home improvement center and visited the paint aisle? How many people did you see scrutinizing all those different shades of beige? Yes, making even a simple choice can be very difficult for some of us. And when the decisions are potentially life-changing, the whole process gets even more intense.

Thankfully, there is a God-given way to simplify the often agonizing decision-making process—a way to navigate that led Ruth through the wilderness and into the Promised Land. It's very much like the method I used to get out of the woods one night.

LOST IN LIFE

The western edge of New York's Adirondack Mountains was known to the local Native American tribes as the *Couxsachrage*. The literal translation means "dismal wilderness." They said it was "too far, too steep, too cold," and so they didn't visit there often or stay long when they did. It is mother earth's homely wild child, a place as difficult to navigate as its Native American name is to pronounce. It is a lonely land that was formed by a drunken glacier, sculpting her into an ugly jungle of back country with crooked bogs and miles of tangled brush, a disheveled hodgepodge of slouching peaks separated by dense blotches of spruce and alder trees. Hip-deep snows in the winter fill hundreds of lonely ponds. Unbroken days of rain in the short summers create a chronically soggy world that breeds legions of angry mosquitoes and black flies that harass fair-weather suitors, chasing them back into their SUVs.

Glamour shots on the covers of brochures and Web pages lure occasional vacationers, but one face-to-face visit is usually enough to end the relationship. Her availability, the lack of competition for her few attractions, is what I found so attractive. A half-hour hike off any road or trail and I could enjoy her undivided attention. I hunted and fished there often and spent days on end wandering around in her and never found the candy wrappers and toilet paper that defile the ground of more attractive destinations. As you can now imagine, it's also the kind of place that one can quickly and easily get lost in. So in an attempt to keep that from happening, I carried a map, two compasses and a not always reliable sense of direction.

My favorite hunting spot was in a relatively open stand of old growth cherry trees that grew along the edge of a steep hillside, running down to a large shallow pond. Under normal conditions, it took about an hour to hike up there from the road where I parked my pickup. The short hours of daylight during the November deer hunting season often made getting back to my truck in the evening a real adventure. As darkness fell, familiar landmarks faded into the gloom. Squalls of cold rain or wet snow blew in unannounced and made it impossible to see more than 50 yards ahead. Trail blazes and strips of surveying tape I had hung on tree branches along the route brought me great comfort, especially on those nights when I stayed a bit longer than I should have. Hearing my pickup truck engine roar to life sounded better than hearing my favorite old song on the radio.

One afternoon in particular stands out in my memory. I was actually heading out a bit earlier than usual, attempting to follow and explore an unfamiliar game trail that started off in the general southeasterly direction I needed to be traveling in. For a half mile or so, the trail continued to take me in the right direction, but then it turned to follow a peat bog running in a northeasterly direction. I followed the path for another half a mile or so thinking there would be a convenient spot to resume my southeasterly trek. Being a male, I am psychologically incapable of turning around, so I instinctively pressed on, hoping, and then eventually praying, that the bog would end so I could turn and cut a beeline southeast toward the logging road which led back to my truck.

It was growing darker by the minute; the bog had no end in sight, and so it was time to make a decision. I could either stop, start a fire and spend a long cold but safe night in the forest—which was the smart thing to do—or I could try to cut directly across the bog and then move as quickly as possible in hopes of making it to the road before nightfall.

Predictably, I decided to attempt crossing the bog. Fortunately, it did not completely swallow me, and I was able to scramble up the rise on the other side. Unfortunately, the rocky hillside gave way to an impossibly dense thicket of small spruce trees. These trees averaged about six feet in height and were growing so closely together that I had to exert quite a bit of energy just to push though the first few feet of them. In a small clearing, I took a moment to catch my breath, dump cold water out of my boots and take a new bearing with my compass. I laced up my boots, double-knotted them and headed southeast toward the road I was hoping was still somewhere out there.

Survival manuals instruct lost persons to stop, sit down and breathe deeply if they lose their way—a relaxation exercise meant to combat the panic accompanying the realization that they might be lost. That's a nice idea, but rarely heeded by those experiencing this primordial fear. Stories of lost hikers and hunters are replete with accounts of bizarre behaviors and foolish decisions made under the influence of this intoxicating panic. It's not uncommon for rescuers to find the bodies of lost people completely naked; their insanity was so complete these lost souls took off all their clothes even in subzero weather. Others are discovered hiding from the search and rescue squads that are trying to save them.

On that evening, I felt those first twinges of panic, and it turned me into a frightened wilderness fullback. Instead of sitting down, I put my head down and plowed through the underbrush. I stiff-armed branches, hurdled logs and crawled my way under heaps of blown-down trees that were blocking my way. The darkening forest sprouted thousands of needled hands that clutched at my clothes as they attempted to spin me into hopeless disorientation. Low branches lashed my face and stole my tuque. The scorned forest turned into a vengeful gauntlet that tripped, taunted and teased. Huffing and puffing, lathered in sweat, I struggled on, stumbling forward in the fading light.

Then I came to a stream and exhaled a big sigh of relief. I knew right then I would be eating dinner with my family and sleeping in my own warm bed that night. Water runs downhill, and that gorgeous little rill was flowing southeast. I followed it closely, enjoying the last hint of daylight reflecting off its surface. The now pitch-black forest pressed down from all sides, so I nervously clung to the edge of that little stream all the way down the hillside and was never more than a few feet away from its comforting gurgle.

Suddenly, I was standing on the logging road; the hard surface slowed my racing heart. I knelt and kissed the ground like the Pope does when he gets off a plane. (A friend told me he does this because he is very afraid of flying.) I was just glad to be out of the woods.

It's pretty easy to get turned around in the wilderness. The GPS you received for Christmas can leave you really lost if you don't learn how to use it, or the battery dies, or you drop it in the lake. Even with the latest geological survey map and high quality compass, it's possible to become disoriented for a little while. Bearings must be adjusted for the variation between magnetic north and true north, and sometimes it's too dark to see what the compass is saying. Even those aerial maps don't tell us exactly how deep that blessed bog is standing directly in the way of our intended route. The good news is there are always two directions that are easy to know—up and down. Unlike the 360 points of the compass, up and down are just two directions, thus eliminating 358 directional options. Sometimes, all we can know is whether we are ascending or descending; it's the bi-directional method of navigation that got me out of the woods that night.

It's also easy to get turned around in life; hundreds of options and directions make us unsure of where we are and where we are supposed to be. Life has a way of spinning our directional compasses. We want to make right decisions. We want to know that the person we marry is God's choice for us. We want to know that the offers we accept and the places we live are God's will for our lives. Yet, in spite of our most earnest attempts at making perfect directional decisions, we often experience confusion and indecision.

Somewhere during my journey with the Lord, I've learned that up and down are the only two directions I need to know. Up is closer to Jesus, down is closer to . . . well, everything that is not Jesus. Having just two directions makes things much simpler. I've also learned that is the surest way of getting to the place God wants us to be.

PROXIMITY'S NAVIGATION

"But Ruth clung to her" is a prophetic picture of people who navigate by clinging to Christ. *"Where you go I shall go"* is the directional orientation guiding all His followers. Like Ruth, they vow to give up the right to decide where they live, what language they speak, even what religion they practice. Ruth becomes the prototype of a distinctly spiritual people who have escaped the tyranny of geography and schedules for the freedom of following Christ. Such people no longer fret over what their address will be as long as He is in the house. These understand that who they are with is infinitely more important than where they reside. The city, the school, the career, all the particulars of life become virtually irrelevant once they determine whose neck they are hanging on. Proximity to Him becomes the final arbiter in all decisions and directions.

This is the exchange of compass, map or GPS for the altimeter of proximity. This endows us with an infallible sense of direction. Paul was referring to this bi-directional orientation when he wrote to the church in Philippi: *"Forgetting what lies behind and reaching forward to what lies ahead, I press on toward the goal for the prize of the upward call of God in Christ Jesus"* (Phil. 3:13-14). Paul lived in a two-direction world, the black-and-white simplicity of pushing forward and upward to be close to his Lord.

When I'm seeking to know the right direction for my life, I apply this same principle. When I get confused or turned around and don't know which way to go, I get closer to Him. I ask myself, *Am I moving toward Him or away from Him?* I look at the altimeter of relationship to determine whether I'm ascending closer to Him or retreating down the path and just letting gravity have its way with me. It's not rocket science, so even someone like me can figure out how to get out of the woods at night!

This is the same kind of directional predicament Ruth was in. Israel and

Bethlehem were just the names of places she had heard of and never been to. Yet inside of this future bride of Boaz was that spiritual altimeter, an irresistible directional pull to follow Naomi, the representative of the Lord. In spite of the lack of blessing, negative self-talk and the dark cloud that was hanging over Naomi's life, the Spirit of God was drawing this young woman through her mother-in-law. Somehow, Ruth knew that if she clung to Naomi she would find the place on the map where she belonged.

If you Google Moab, you'll learn that it is a mountainous place, so Ruth and Naomi descended as they began their journey to cross the Jordan Valley and re-cross the border into the Promised Land. They would have started back up as they climbed the hills into Bethlehem. But make no mistake about it; in spite of the ups and downs along the route, their journey was uphill all the way. So too is following Christ. The gravitational attraction of our carnal nature to the earth insures that every step we take closer to Him is an uphill one. Using the altimeter of relationship as our primary directional aid will be kind of scary at first and will take some getting used to.

Where we will go to school, who we will marry, what job we will take and who we will be accountable to are all very important questions we need to ask. Amid hundreds of directional options, we earnestly try to read tea leaves of circumstances and attempt to hear the Lord through the din of opinions and prophecies. Like Gideon, we will even set out our own secret fleeces in our quest to get the correct coordinates. Yet, in spite of all our honest efforts, these conflicting feelings and swirling opinions settle in like a thick fog. We ask our friends for prayer and pray that prophets will call us out from the crowd and give us a specific word telling us who, what, when and where. The harder we try to know the right thing to do, the faster the needles of our compasses seem to spin. I believe God allows them to spin because He wants us to learn how to discern direction, make decisions and view the course of our lives in this altogether different way.

This is why learning to trust His presence in our decision-making is definitely a process. It is a different level of trust when we trust Him to take care of not only our eternal souls, but to also lead us in the here-and-now world of places and people. Surrendering the right to self-determination is difficult;

it is unnatural to be led by His presence. Our Adamic inclination is to know where we are going before we set off and to make logical decisions based on the data we have gathered. Yet, in spite of our best natural efforts, when the hour of decision comes upon us, we often flounder about like contestants on a game show who must choose while the audience shouts its unintelligible advice. Then, once the decision is made, we still question if the person lying in bed next to us was God's perfect choice for us. We spend the best hours of our days and the best years of our lives working hard and still wonder if we've heard correctly from God when we signed the contract.

Thankfully, He is progressively leading us to a place where we are free from the tyranny and terror of having to make perfect decisions while under the stress of life. Over time, we learn to accept that, as long as we are holding His hand, we will always choose the door He wants us to walk through. What's behind the door begins to not seem as important as it once did. We come to believe the proverb that says, "The man who walks with God will always reach his destination." In His presence, the tension and stress of decision-making and course-setting melt away. Our plan is to walk as closely to Him as we can without conditions or reservations; it's a simple plan.

Bi-directional orientation also releases us from the vicissitude and bondage of the hyper-spiritual claim that we have heard directly from God in every decision we have made; in reality, we have simply sewn the label of God's will on our own fleeces in hopes of a happy and successful outcome in all our endeavors. I'm often perplexed by folks who claim that God has spoken to them about so many of the details of their lives. I know God speaks to us, and so I don't have a problem with that. What perplexes me is how often God appears to change His mind. Funny how His mind seems to change when things don't go like we planned or hoped.

It's comforting for me to know that this was the same deal offered to the disciples. When they asked, *"'Where are You staying?'"* He did not give them a street address, but said *"'Come and you will see'"* (John 1:39). He walked past their homes and businesses and said, *"Follow Me'"* (John 1:43). Jesus never separated mission from relationship; He never separated our final destination from proximity to Himself. Today, He offers us the same opportunity He offered His first followers to join Him on His journey.

Think of it as a first-class seat on Kingdom Airlines. We get on board without knowing where we are going. We find our seats, snap our safety belts, and a voice comes over the public address system. "This is Captain Jesus. I'm so glad you chose to fly Kingdom Air. Our destination today is transformation, and we will be arriving when we get there. So sit back and enjoy the flight, and remember all Kingdom Air flights are non-smoking." The engines roar, we are pushed back on our seats, and we are off to parts unknown.

I believe the primary reason He rarely gives us the coordinates of our final destination or the specifics of our task is because that information would tempt us to make the journey without Him. Most of us are already nervous about flying on Kingdom Air; there are just too many unknowns. We like the Captain and all, but some of the other passengers are pretty sketchy. As a matter of fact, it's hard to believe they even let them through security. So we would be tempted to hop a bus or take the train and just reconnect with Him when we got there. But, of course, being right with the Lord is not like finding the X on the map. What happens to us in route is every bit as critical as where we end up. This is why I've given up hounding Him about the details of my life. I'm just along for the ride.

For me, being at the right place at the right time is no longer the goal; it is the inevitable consequence of being with Him. Moses was given a cloud by day and pillar of fire by night, not a map of the Middle East with some circles and arrows. Clinging to Him means you're in the right place all the time. He's not coaxing us into some dark wilderness to abandon us. In fact, He often calls us to some wild places so we can be with Him. And we can be rest assured that, when we do find ourselves in the wilderness, it is because that is where He is.

ASSURANCE OF GUIDANCE

Bi-directional orientation also releases us from the vicissitude and bondage of interpreting the correctness of decisions according to their initial outcomes or levels of comfort we experience. My experience has taught me that, more often than not, being at His side means things are going to go well. I've learned this because most of my life has been lived under some very blue skies. With that said, I'm also aware that not all decisions take us down the easiest path each and every time. Both personal histories and Biblical accounts are replete with examples of folks who made correct decisions, yet from all appearances their choices did not look like such good decisions.

Do you think Ruth ever regretted her decision to cling to Naomi and follow her back to Bethlehem? For her, the decision to leave Moab was a stroke of pure genius. It was the decision that wrote her "she-lived-happily-ever-after" epitaph. The real question we should ask is, would Ruth's decision to follow Naomi back to Bethlehem have been wrong if everything had not worked out so well? What if she did not get to marry her redeemer prince?

I love traditional wedding vows; as a pastor, I encourage couples to use them as often as I can. The weighty words, "for better for worse, for richer or poorer in sickness and in health," echo the timeless sentiments of our covenantal relationship with our Redeemer and His covenantal relationship with us, His Bride. I especially enjoy wedding services that include Ruth's words, *"for where you go, I will go, and where you lodge, I will lodge. Your people shall be my people, and your God, my God."* All these words eloquently capture this truth that situation and circumstance cannot be the final arbiters of relationship and decision-making.

This is how Jesus was led during His life here on earth. He was led by the Spirit into the wilderness, and He was led to Jerusalem to die. This assurance of guidance that flowed from intimate relationship with the Father allowed Him to face temptation without thinking, *I must have missed Him.* It allowed Him to walk down the *Via Dolorosa*, the path of grief, without feeling like he took a wrong turn somewhere. The Father's words over Him at His baptism were words of relationship: *"'This is my beloved Son in whom I am well pleased'"* (Matt. 3:17). Not "Here is where You need to go and what You need to do over the next three years of Your ministry . . . ."

Being led by His presence is part of the mystery and romance of Divine relationship; He beckons us to follow Him down paths and up slopes on which we have never been. He presses forward up the trail. He entices us to journey with Him into the unknown. In quiet moments, we sit with Him along the way and ask where we are going. He smiles and says, "Just stay close. You'll see," and we're off again. We walk with Him into the splendor of His Kingdom; we camp in dewy pastures and follow meandering streams in lonely places. We follow until we have no idea where we are and no longer care. Each day is an adventure in an unexplored and unknown world with the Lover of our souls, a place where we have only the abiding presence of His rod and staff to guide and comfort us. In the high pastures, we catch glimpses of what will be, places so elevated that the daily issues of life appear in their true size. It's a wilderness where we never feel lost and where we are assured of His guidance.

CHAPTER 5
Bitterness

*"And she said, 'Do not call me Naomi; call me Mara,
for the Almighty has dealt very bitterly with me. I went out full, but the Lord
has brought me back empty. Why do you call me Naomi, since the Lord has
witnessed against me and the Almighty has afflicted me?'"* (RUTH 1:20-21).

Naomi was a bitter woman. She is a prophetic image of a generation that
has imbibed deeply from the glass of bitterness. She greeted her old
friends and neighbors back in Bethlehem with an honest yet caustic
description of her life: *"No longer call me Naomi; call me Mara, for the Almighty has dealt very bitterly with me"* (Ruth 1:20).

The tragedy and heartbreak of her journey had left its mark on her soul.
She believed herself cursed by the Almighty and cut off from the blessings of
her faith. Moreover, she was not going to allow her plight to be glossed over
by her well-wishers and friends. She was angry, bitter, and everyone in that
religious community was going to know about it! In other words, she was
really saying, "God is not good and all of you pew warmers are going to know
about it, and don't give me any of your religious platitudes and mumbo
jumbo about a good God who loves me and has a plan for my life . . . I've
seen His plan, and it sucks!"

Indeed, Naomi had drunk from a cup of bitter spirits. Absinthe is a bitter spirit. According to Wikipedia, absinthe was the drink of choice for many
in the artistic and literary community that Vincent Van Gogh was a part of
in the late nineteenth century.[1] Undoubtedly, its popularity was due largely to
its perceived, but not necessarily proven, hallucinogenic properties that its
consumers believed to inspire them in their creative endeavors and, at times,
thought to provoke them to do crazy things. Take Van Gogh, for example.
He cut off part of his ear and sent it to a prostitute. You may have heard about

this famous artist's bizarre behavior, but what you may not know is that he was under the influence of absinthe. Another curious thing about Van Gogh is he fervently wanted to be in the Christian ministry, so much so that he served as a missionary in his youth. Religion, we will discover, does not insure sane behavior.

WORMWOOD

Absinthe's primary ingredient, according to Wikipedia, is distilled from *Artemisia absinthium*, commonly known as grande wormwood or absinthe wormwood. Two other herbs, anise and fennel, are usually combined to create the light green drink which is sometimes referred to as the "The Green Fairy." Interestingly, these three herbs most commonly used to concoct this drink are called the "Holy Trinity."[2]

There are more than 120 species in the genus of plants commonly known as wormwood. Some of these plants have medicinal value, but they are primarily known for their extremely bitter taste. In several places, the Bible uses wormwood to describe how bitter something or someone is. Deuteronomy 29:18 prohibits the presence of anyone whose heart is turned against the Lord—*"lest there shall be among you a root bearing poisonous fruit and wormwood."* This same language is used in the New Testament letter to the Hebrews where the church is admonished to be diligent not to allow a *"root of bitterness springing up"* that *"causes trouble, and by it many be defiled"* (Heb. 12:15).

In Proverbs 5:4, the adulterous woman is described as being as bitter as wormwood. In Revelation, a great star known as Wormwood falls upon a third of the springs and rivers, and *"many men died from the waters, because they were made bitter"* (Rev. 8:11). These all are sober warnings printed on the bottle of wormwood about the potentially deadly consequences of ingesting the toxic brew of bitterness.

Being bitter is not sin; it's a spiritual condition caused by sin. Being bitter is not sin; it's a spiritual condition caused by sin. This is not a typographical error. I've repeated this sentence to get your attention. All too often we attempt to remedy the symptoms of bitterness the same way we address sin.

Unfortunately, the symptoms continue to erupt because the root of the problem, the source of the bitterness, does not get treated. Like those pesky dandelions in the lawn that keep growing back no matter how often we chop off their flowers, bitterness grows back because its roots go deep.

The sins of others, our own sins or the circumstances of life conspire together and poison our spirits. The sin bitter people usually participate in is their unwillingness to be treated. Bitter people certainly have things they can repent from; we all do. Being a victim does not absolve us of our duty to take responsibility for things others have said and done while under the influence of this toxin. Bitterness is Satan's way of killing off those whom he has already robbed and destroyed; it's the poison's residue left in the body long after the painful events occurred.

Wormwood has three chemical properties or characteristics that make these plants poignant examples of bitterness toward God and His people. This is why the Scriptures use these plants to illustrate the specific nature of bitterness. These three attributes are the bitter taste, the water solubility of the toxins and the hallucinogenic influence of ingestion. The latter property has come into question in more recent years, but it's definitely characteristic of bitterness.

If you've experienced bitterness, either in yourself or in someone you are close to, I trust these observations will lead you to seek out the only effective antidote for this deadly spiritual condition. My prayer is that you will find the One who is the antidote to this deadly toxin.

TASTE

To my knowledge, which I admit may be limited, nothing naturally poisonous tastes good. This is why assassins in the movies always have to mix the poison into a yummy drink, and when their intended victim is not looking, they quickly switch glasses. Apparently, God has hardwired humankind's pallets to detect poisons by the simple test of taste. Blackberries and mangos taste great, and they are good for you. The only exception to this general rule would have been the tree of the knowledge of good and evil. But for modern man living in this post-Edenic world, it's a simple and effective test that has served mankind well. If it tastes good, you can eat it; if it's bitter, you might want to dump it out into a potted plant when your host is not looking.

Our souls also have taste, a very similar and innate ability to detect bitter from sweet and, therefore, poisonous from edible. From time to time, we will encounter people who are full of bitterness. We ask them what is wrong or inquire how they are doing when we observe their contorted faces and pained expressions. These innocent questions lance their emotional and spiritual wounds that are just waiting to be vented. When the floodgates of decorum that normally keep the putrid waters of bitterness dammed up actually open up, watch out! The spewing forth of disillusionment, anger and frustration lets loose like a bad case of verbal dysentery. It is our natural instinct to recoil from it.

It's more than probable that the number of visitors to Naomi and Ruth's place dramatically declined once they were exposed to Naomi's sentiments. Like the denizens of Bethlehem, we too can taste the poison of bitterness. No matter how badly we feel for our poisoned friends, we know that for the sake of our own health and the health of our families we must severely curtail the amount of time we spend listening to or reading the words of these poisoned individuals.

Bitterness of the soul cannot be assuaged by human understanding and compassion. From the victim's perspective, he has valid reasons for his bitterness even as Naomi did. She had buried her husband and two sons in foreign soil; she was impoverished and getting on in years. She was bitter and had a right to be so. If you've ever sat down and attempted to talk someone out of her bitterness, then you already know the futility of this endeavor. We find ourselves trying to defend God and explain the mystery of pain and suffering in the universe to someone who has already passed judgment on Him. The taste is unmistakable.

Offense is the first leg in the journey to bitterness. Have you ever noticed that we only get offended with people who we believe should and can do something for us? If I make an announcement in church that I need help moving a piano next Saturday morning, and on that next Saturday morning no one shows up, I'm not offended with the 70-year-old saints; I'm offended with the 20-year-old studs that slept in or stayed home to play Xbox that morning.

Our unmet expectations and subsequent offense open up fissures in our souls that the root of bitterness grows into. All of us have reason to be offended with someone, even God. This is why no one is immune to the toxins of bitterness. We get offended with God the "Almighty," as Naomi sarcastically calls Him, the One who should help and can help and chooses to stay in heaven. He stays out of our personal Moabs. Because we interpret our suffering as His witness against us, it seems like the only way to dull the pain of our cursed existence is to become drunk on the soul-numbing and mind-altering booze of bitterness.

This is why churches and other religious organizations are so rife with offense and bitterness. It's one of the few social institutions where our expectations about how others should treat us are so clearly defined and so often unmet from our myopic perspective. It's the place where we affirm our belief in an omnipotent and benevolent God and yet live in the incomplete actualization of His promises. Combined with the demonic influences that are seeking to exacerbate and inflame our offenses with one another, we have a milieu that is perfect for growing the nasty-tasting root of bitterness. Offense quickly ripens into bitterness in the shadows of the mildewed church cellar full of whispers, suspicions and innuendo.

Don't tell anyone, but I heard from someone (I can't say whom) that religions and their institutional structures are not an antidote for the poison of bitterness. Not only that, but I also heard that there are lots of people (I can't mention whom) who are probably going to leave because the pastor was not able to help Naomi. But let's just keep this between us.

WATER SOLUBLE

The chemicals in wormwood are dissolved by water. When it rains, the toxins in wormwood dissolve and drip off the plant, poisoning the ground around it. In one of those amazing novelties of the natural world, these bitter plants produce their own water-soluble herbicide. They kill off or stunt the plants near them that are competing for light, water and nutrition.

Bitterness and offense are not private affairs; they drip off one soul and have the potential to poison everyone who comes near. In Hebrews 12:15, the passage about bitterness includes a warning about *"many [being] defiled"* because bitter people will contaminate those around them. The only kinds of plants that can grow around them are other bitter plants. Bitter people seem to thrive in the presence of one another; the bitterness and offense are weeds that spread rapidly. Therefore, the Lord is committed to their eradication.

Bitterness creates both desire and loathing for human interaction. Bitter people want others to know about their pain just like Naomi did. There is no point in having a spiritual temper tantrum if no one is around to see it. While bitter individuals want people to watch their fits, they don't want anyone interfering with their right to have one and reject any attempt to intervene. Our friends who have been sickened by bitterness may attract a few well-meaning individuals who want to help them recover. But these kind folks are usually quickly overwhelmed by the severity of the problem. At this point in the disease's progression, experts are usually called in to attempt to remedy the problem.

Historically, we know that Rabbinic Judaism had not yet emerged during this era of judges; rabbis are the trained leaders of local synagogues where Jews meet each Sabbath. Yet, I think it safe to assume that elders and other local spiritual leaders in Bethlehem would have been called in to bring their expertise to bear on the problem. They would have gladly visited Naomi at the bequest of well-meaning but overwhelmed friends and neighbors who were deeply concerned for the emotional, spiritual and even physical welfare of their old friend. Clergy and other spiritual leaders are often the targets of angry transference because of their perceived representation of the One who can do anything, yet who is choosing to do nothing to relieve the pain and suffering of the afflicted soul. Unfortunately, expert advice and accurate diagnosis are not a cure.

Naomi's return to Bethlehem was greeted with amazement, curiosity and any number of well-wishers and friends who would have stopped by for a visit and offered some assistance. We know that *the whole city was stirred because of them*" (Ruth 1:19). Surely, some of Naomi's and Elimelech's old friends would have said something like, "Naomi, if there is anything we can do for you, please let us know . . . it's good to have you back here again . . . we're so sorry for your loss." The door to reenter the life of this community was open, yet apparently Naomi was unwilling and, therefore, unable to walk through it.

Naomi's sudden venting of her bitterness undoubtedly shocked them. I imagine a tight-knit community like Bethlehem would have responded with gifts of food and meals that rural communities everywhere are famous for. My suspicion is that no matter how magnanimously the community responded to Naomi, she would have still been bitter. Her beef ultimately was with God. Casseroles and flowers were not going to bring her family back from the dead. In the end, she would have to face the Almighty. In the meantime, the community was going to withdraw from her because no one can come close to a bitter person without being poisoned herself.

HALLUCINOGENIC

What do you do when you get an ear in the mail? Scream, vomit and call the police? We can be quite certain that even the wise Dear Abby doesn't know the proper social etiquette for such a gruesome gift. People do insane and hurtful things when they are under the influence of drugs, especially drugs that cause them to hallucinate. They see things that don't exist, they hear things that were never said, and they do things that hurt themselves and those around them.

Bitterness is such a drug. This is why Naomi says that she *"went out full."* In reality, she actually she went out empty. Her family left the Promised Land during a time of famine. Unfortunately, her ability to see and remember clearly was impaired by bitterness.

When we are under the influence of bitterness, we see conspiracies where there are none and are convinced we have heard people say things that they didn't say. Like Naomi, we don't remember things accurately. That's why a bitter person can't be reasoned with—he is incapable of discerning the real world from the imaginary world created by the green fairy of bitterness, the psychotropic influence of the toxin that courses through his spiritual veins. Until the toxin is out of his system, there is little even our Christian community can do. What is left for us is prayer—prayer for the bitter to allow the Healer to touch his soul. Sadly, even the friends of the inebriated often get accused of being part of the problem, taking sides, not listening or not caring. Bitterness can make us so delirious that we don't know whom to trust.

Bitterness can even induce us to hurt ourselves. Like Van Gough, the bitter person is often willing to mutilate or destroy herself to make her point. It is a form of suicidal spiritual protest. We douse ourselves in gas and incinerate ourselves publicly on the steps of the temple to draw attention to our plight. It's a hunger strike against man and God, where we are willing to starve ourselves to death rather than give up our anger. It's very likely that Naomi's unwillingness to glean was evidence of her willingness to die rather than receive the cure for her pain. She, like all bitter souls, would have known that detoxing from bitterness included forgiving the debts owed her. We and she blindly cling to the false hope of repayment. We hold the gun to our own heads, trying to rough up our debtors with guilt, a mistaken and futile attempt to coerce them to settle their account with us.

Neither does the passage of time correct our vision. In fact, if anything, the years seem to ferment the bitterness into an even more potent toxin. I feel sorry for the kindly, sweet-hearted seniors who are languishing alone in facilities that take care of them until death carries them away. Visiting nursing homes is a rewarding and wonderful ministry to folks who still need love and human contact from the outside world. Unfortunately, some older folks don't have many visitors because their bitterness has made it so difficult for their friends and family to associate with them. Visitors get lectured, yelled at, belittled and berated whenever they come around. The bitterness in their souls, like that which was in Naomi's, remains as virile as ever, even as their bodies succumb to the inevitable weakening of old age.

Being diagnosed with bitterness is not easy to accept; it feels like a slam, an impugning of our character. Like hearing any bad news from the doctor, there is sure to be the normal range of emotions—denial, anger and shock, all of that. Of course, we need to accept the diagnosis before we will receive the cure.

Perhaps you can relate to Naomi. Maybe you, too, have tasted of spiritual wormwood. Could it be her actions and words resonate in your soul? I'd ask you to prayerfully consider the very real possibility that you may be embittered toward man or God. Naomi's story is a sober warning to us, if we'll receive it, about this potentially deadly condition.

Up until this point, I've endeavored to follow the chronological order of Ruth's story. I believe it's needful here to offer God's antitoxin for the gall of bitterness. And although in Ruth's book we don't learn of the antivenin until the end of the story, in our next chapter in this text, we will explain God's cure for this condition, His remedy for that which man has no medicine.

CHAPTER 6
Antivenin

"Then the women said to Naomi, 'Blessed is the Lord who has not left you without a redeemer today . . . .' Then Naomi took the child and laid him in her lap, and became his nurse. And the neighbor women gave him a name, saying, 'A son has been born to Naomi!' So they named him Obed. He is the father of Jesse, the father of David" (RUTH 4:14-17).

Being healed from bitterness is a Holy Spirit-guided process. Much like the healing of a physical disease or injury, it follows a predictable pattern of diagnosis, remedy and rehabilitation.

Remember bitterness is not a sin; it's a symptom. Bitterness is the lingering and often debilitating consequence of sin and evil that plagues us and the world we live in. The good news is that it is completely treatable. There is both a cure and rehabilitation for those who have experienced this toxin of the soul.

THE CURE

Instituto Clodomiro Picado is a scientific institute located in San Pedro, Costa Rica, that specializes in the development of antivenin. With 13 species of poisonous snakes, this tiny nation has vested interest in curing snakebites! Antivenin is derived from animal blood rich in antibodies that neutralize the venom of these often deadly snakes. Cloromiro Picado, a Costa Rican scientist, pioneered the techniques that supply the medical community with effective antidotes for most of the world's venomous snakes.[3] The way in which antivenin is produced provides us with some insights as to how God has produced His own antivenin for humanity.

After the poisonous snakes are caught, they are "milked." Expert snake handlers carefully press the fangs of the snakes into rubber sheeting stretched over a collection beaker. The venom is involuntarily released by the snake, and the milk is collected by the scientist. Small amounts of the venom are then injected into a host animal. About every ten days, increasing amounts of venom are injected into the host which enables the animal to produce increasing amounts of antibodies that saturate its blood. After three or four months, there are enough antibodies to use this blood for the production of antivenin. During the process, the animal itself becomes immune to the snake venom. Eventually, the antibody-rich serum of the animal's blood is processed into antivenin that can save the lives of countless numbers of snakebite victims.

The first animals that Dr. Picado used to produce antivenin were horses. Their large size made them good candidates for the process. Unfortunately, the blood of horses would frequently be rejected by the human immune system and made the antivenin less effective. What was eventually discovered was that sheep were better animals to use in the production of antivenin. Sheep's blood was much less likely to be rejected by the human immune system, and today sheep are the animal of choice in the production of antivenin. Poison injected into a sheep causes the blood of the sheep to become the cure for a serpent's bite. Does that sound familiar in some way to you? It does to me.

Remember the serpent in Eden? The first human's disobedience exposed their soft flesh to his venom (Gen. 3:1), and he did not miss his opportunity to strike. His fangs injected sin into Adam, and every generation since has suffered the horrible consequences.

Sin-tainted blood transmits rebellion into each successive generation; each infant born into the world is born with the poison of sin locked in his or her spiritual blood. Humankind cannot heal itself. There is no miracle cure for sin's poison locked in an exotic plant deep in the endangered rainforest. There's no regimen of diet and exercise that can purge our blood of this toxin. No amount of pious prayer, fasting or sacrificial good works can ever reverse the consequences of Satan's bite. No counseling, psychoanalysis or advice will remedy this condition that plagues humanity.

The antidote for sin is the blood of Jesus Christ. The Father allowed Satan to bite His Son on the Cross, where he injected the Lamb of God with the sin, shame and bitterness of every human who ever lived. For six hours, venom was injected into the Lamb of God in one massive and fatal overdose.

He was bitten, and He died. There was no antivenin in the world that could cure His fatal wounds. For three days, His heart stopped beating. For three days, His body received no oxygen, His body cooled, His brain waves stopped. *"He made Him who knew no sin to be sin on our behalf . . ."* (2 Cor. 5:21). For three days, the divine remedy for every malady that plagues humanity remained bottled in the near-eastern earth. Then, the cork popped!

Jesus rose from the dead, resurrected to eternal life. His holy blood—humanity's antivenin created in heaven and delivered to earth—is now available to every sin-sick son of Adam. The serpent's poison finally had a cure—the remedy injected by faith, the personal recognition of His divine nature and substitutionary death. And it was freely dispensed and joyfully administered to all who call upon His name. I've discovered that I need a fresh transfusion of His blood to cure the continual infestation of toxins I'm infected with. I'm grateful that His blood is always available to me.

REHABILITATION

Like all of God's people living before the incarnation of Christ, Naomi was only able to catch prophetic glimpses of the Messiah who was to come. For Naomi, the infant in her lap was that glimpse. That baby boy was the poultice of hope, drawing out the bitter poison that had made her soul so sick. The infant Obed, born in Bethlehem, in the lineage of David, was the flesh and blood promise that pointed toward the coming of the Boy who was to be born in Bethlehem. Naomi, much like the devout Simeon and the ageless prophetess Anna, was able to see and hold an infant of promise.

The text says that *"Naomi took the child and laid him in her lap"* and became his nurse or caretaker. She became actively involved with the protection and nurture of her grandson. This active involvement with the well-being and care of the next generation of God's people is the rehabilitation that brings complete healing to a disillusioned and embittered generation. The reinvestment of her life into the life of the child Obed is a prophetic image of a senior generation investing into the lives of the freshmen who are soon to take up pivotal position in the ever-expanding Kingdom of God. Naomi takes responsibility and ownership for the success of the next generation and is fully healed from her bitterness in the process.

Rehabilitation and therapy usually involve some pain, just ask someone who has had a hip or knee replaced. He will tell you about pain. Likewise, there must have been some pain, some difficult hurdles for Naomi to clear before she took the step to unreservedly embrace her grandson. I can see at least three difficulties for Naomi to overcome.

First, it's not her flesh and blood. Obed is not related to Naomi by blood. Naomi's two boys Mahlon and Chilion got sick, and they died. Their death meant Naomi and Elimelech's DNA was permanently erased from the human gene pool. For some people, the absence of a genetic connection can be a stumbling point. If for some reason we cannot accept that our own seed, both natural and spiritual, will not inherit the blessing, we could mistakenly hold the next generation at arm's length. We may tolerate stepchildren, but can we fully embrace them? Aloof, unable to embrace those without our genes and family name, we find ourselves emotionally detached from the new thing the Lord is doing while we lament our own offspring's absence.

Ultimately, this lack of support for people and institutions that are not ours is a pride issue. We want our family name, our denomination, our spiritual heritage to be recognized and esteemed. The proper response to pride is honesty and humility. We need to honestly appraise the health of our legacy and humbly recognize our own mistakes. When we rightly acknowledge that God is sovereign and that we are His servants, we will be able to embrace whomever and whatever He blesses. If we fail to do this, we will be forever covering up the weaknesses and mistakes of those we want to inherit the blessings.

A poignant example of this kind of unhealthy family allegiance is seen in the life of the priest Eli (1 Sam. 2-4). He continued to mistakenly endorse his sons' ministry as priests, in spite of knowing they had disqualified themselves from leadership because of their immoral conduct. Eli had a blind spot when it came to his sons, and his failure to rebuke and discipline them brought a reproach to the priesthood and ended with the sudden and violent death of both father and sons with his mantle of blessing falling on Samuel.

A second potential difficulty could arise because the next generation is a bit foreign to us. It seems inevitable that some of Ruth's Moabite culture would have rubbed off on Obed. Lullabies, language, customs and mannerisms don't fade in a single generation. Cultural norms are forever shifting and changing. Embracing and nurturing the next generation means embracing things that are foreign to us, things that make us uncomfortable, or simply rub us the wrong way. I'm sure Naomi was irritated or bothered more than once by the things little Obed learned from his mother.

If we cannot or will not embrace foreign things, we will not fulfill God's purpose for our lives. If our homes and churches become sanctuaries for our cultures, then very few foreign babies will ever find their way onto our laps. The plastic covers on the furniture, untouchable relics, nervous glances and stern warnings can make grandmother's house a place no one wants to visit. I wonder how many things Obed broke when he was a kid? I wonder if he ever peed on the rug or pooped on the bed? Wonder if he sang some songs Naomi didn't like and used expressions she didn't really understand? Sure glad she didn't let any of those things stand in the way of taking care of that boy.

A final place of challenge for Naomi could have been his size and age. Obed is an infant when Naomi starts to invest in his life. Changing diapers and wiping chins may not seem like important work at the time, but they are. Naomi might have been tempted to wait until the boy was older before she started to participate in his life. It's actually a pretty common misconception to think that the influence and impartation can only begin once the person or institution has reached a certain size or level of maturity. It's one of the reasons teaching children is so rewarding. Teaching children means we get to sow spiritual seed in unplanted soil; we get to work in the wet concrete of youth.

Important and meaningful communication does not suddenly erupt when our daughters have their first crush or our sons have their first fight. The paths of communication are worn in bit by bit; we walk in and out of our children's lives over the well-worn paths that were blazed by seemingly inconsequential conversations about teachers, pets and the weather. The daughter who wants to talk about her lost doll is the same child who will want to talk about her first boyfriend. The young man you help fix his car stereo is the same young man who will ask you whether he should go to college, join the military or take a year off to go to the mission field.

HEALED OR OLD AGE

The women of Bethlehem pronounce blessing over Naomi's life, and she does not protest as she did when she first returned. She is silent as they say, *"Blessed is the Lord who has not left you without a redeemer today, and may his name become famous in Israel. May he also be to you a restorer of life and sustainer of your old age . . ."* (Ruth 4:14-15).

This reference to her age is critical in any discussion about bitterness in the Body of Christ. We all are aware that certain sicknesses or diseases are most common among certain age groups. Pediatricians are trained to know the diseases of childhood, and gerontologists know the problems of old age. While bitterness can afflict us at any age, it seems most common and acute with older generations. As the idealism of youth is swallowed up by the pragmatism of middle age, we all become more vulnerable to its toxin. As dreams and visions are replaced by disappointments and failures, it's easy, almost natural, to allow our souls to become intoxicated by wormwood's evil cocktail.

Our final picture of Naomi is with Obed on her lap. This is her legacy, her life's message. Maybe you can see her in your mind's eye? Imagine an older woman making silly faces at a pudgy baby, his toothless grin inviting her to perform ever sillier antics as he tossed giggles and drool in her soul's hat.

Their eyes meet, his miniature hand touches her face, and he wipes the bitterness off her furrowed brow. Imagine her changing his diaper, smashing his food, mending his clothes, watching him toddle, reading him stories, seeing him play with the neighbor's kids. I'd like to think she went to Obed's wedding; one of his big friends would have helped her get seated down in front where she could see and hear everything. During the service, she would close her eyes, sweet tears sparkling on the old gal's cheeks.

The text says she *"took the child."* She made a decision; she took the initiative to get involved in the nurture of that baby. Here come the neighbor women again, and they pronounce something even more amazing, *"A son has been born to Naomi.'"* The line between mother and grandmother disappears. Again, there is no protest, no denial of ownership. All we know is that Obed grows up to become Jesse's father—mission accomplished.

When Naomi made the decision to take Obed and lay him in her lap, the injuries of bitterness were healed; she became whole again. She needed the next generation. But the next generation needed her, too. I find it interesting that we know nothing about Ruth's role in Obed's life. We are left to speculate if Ruth got so busy with family business she left Obed with Naomi most of the time, or if Ruth got sick or even died in childbirth, we just don't know. But what we do know is that in the earth today there are no shortages of parentless children. Churches seem to have a surplus of prodigal sons and daughters, and our shelves are stocked with older brother types. What we lack are adequate numbers of Naomis, older folks who fully embrace the care of the next generation. My prayer is that God would raise up a Naomi for every Obed—a generation of senior saints who embody the blessing of Psalm 92:12-14—

> *The righteous man will flourish like the palm tree. He will grow like a cedar in Lebanon. Planted in the house of the Lord, they will flourish in the courts of our God. They will still yield fruit in old age; they shall be full of sap and very green.*

Her cooperation with and participation in the opportunity to care for Obed were essential in her deliverance from bitterness. Naomi experienced healing, and thankfully her story does not end with her as a bitter and lonely old soul. She does not finish her years sequestered away from community and family, brooding over the "would've, should've, could've" remorse that seems to be an all too common part of human experience.

No, she receives the cure for her bitterness, the antidote for the poison that has been injected into her soul. Then she participates in the rehabilitation that allows her to reaccept her birth name and becomes a prophetic prototype of individuals who are set free from bitterness. She is a beautiful Scriptural picture of someone who was poisoned, healed and rehabilitated—someone who lived out the rest of her years loving and being loved by her family and community and enjoying the promise and hope that bitterness had stolen from her. This was her redemption. Now, let's get back to Ruth's redemption.

CHAPTER 7
The Right Place

"And Ruth the Moabitess said to Naomi, 'Please let me go to the field and glean among the ears of grain . . . .' And she said to her, 'Go, my daughter.' So she departed and went and gleaned in the field after the reapers; and she happened to come to the portion of the field belonging to Boaz . . ." (RUTH 2:2-3).

R uth wandered into Boaz's field. Of the hundreds, if not thousands, of cultivated acres surrounding Bethlehem, she ended up in the field of the man she would soon marry. Was it coincidence or destiny? Was it providence or happenstance?

Naomi and Ruth correctly interpreted Ruth's discovery as the benevolent providence of God. An unseen hand guided her down the right path, a supernatural internal navigation system told her when and where to turn. She walked into the field of blessing; her feet were guided to the place where God's love would be lavished upon her.

Happening upon the blessings of God remains one of the great thrills of serving Him. I can personally attest to many such occurrences in my own life, but I can remember one time in particular that resulted in a divine encounter.

THE LAST PLACE

After our honeymoon, Neen and I moved to a region with double-digit unemployment. The heavy industries that had brought abundant high-paying manufacturing jobs to the region faltered, and the work migrated to more temperate parts of the country. The economic downturn was accompanied by a social depression that settled into the hearts and souls of the beleaguered population. The help wanted section of the newspaper took up less than a column, wages were cut, and people carefully guarded their existing jobs. I had been warned about the employment situation prior to our relocation but didn't pay much attention to what I thought were exaggerated fears. I had always been able to find work before and assumed finding a job would be no problem.

In late fall, we rented a dilapidated house out in the country. It sported a sink and a shower that drained directly into the basement; the rats that lived down there enjoyed the luxury of running water. We had an indoor toilet that skimmed over with ice when it got really cold and an old oil furnace that spewed soot through the registers whenever it kicked on. So that first winter we heated the drafty place with a not-so-airtight wood stove that went through a face-cord of hard wood faster than a chain smoker went through a carton of Marlboros. When the wind was blowing from the right direction, powdery snow would filter through the kitchen walls and settle on the white Formica countertop. We had lots of blankets and could not have been happier.

On our first Sunday in town, an acquaintance of my wife's hurried over to our pew the instant church concluded. She had heard I would be looking for work and excitedly told me that she knew where I could find a job driving truck. I shrugged off her tip, explaining I didn't want to jump at the first job I found and was planning on being a bit more selective. I was convinced that a sharp young guy like me with a diploma from a non-accredited Bible college could do better than that. She looked confused when I told her I didn't want the contact information or the address of the possible employer.

I was optimistic and full of fiery arrogance as I drove my little blue Toyota pickup into town early that Monday morning. I was sure I would quickly find an exciting, decent paying job that would prove the negative prognostications about finding work to be overinflated fear. I would be able to prove my conservative theories about work even in this frigid and hostile economic laboratory—theories my conservative father taught me, theories postulating the availability of work for anyone who really wanted to work. Yes, he educated me about people without jobs, telling me they didn't really try hard enough to find one. I steered my rusty truck directly into the belly of the economic monster.

Naturally, my first stop was the offices of one of those companies that had recently suffered a layoff of nearly all its employees. The man at the desk thought I was joking and actually laughed out loud when I told him I was looking for a job. Unfazed by this initial rejection, I continued on my search. Incredulous smirks and shaking heads greeted me at all the businesses I visited that day. By noon, after dozens of cold calls, I figured this might take longer than I thought. One guy actually complimented my misguided attempts. He said he hadn't had anyone come looking for work in a couple of years. It was getting dark when I finally admitted defeat and starting heading back home.

On the way out of town, I noticed a Quonset hut with a vinyl-sided office attached to the front; the sign indicated it was a plumbing company. The lights were still on, so I thought, *Why not? One more cast before I reel in and call it a day.* A portly elderly man was washing his hands in a stainless steel sink when I came in. Like all the other people I had encountered that day, he looked surprised when I told him I was looking for a job. But what he said was a shock to me. He told me that his delivery guy had just quit last Friday and he was looking for a temporary employee who would take the guy's place until he sold his business in the spring. He hired me on the spot. The job paid six dollars an hour and included an hour of overtime every day, paying me time and a half. I even got medical benefits. Not exactly the job I was looking for, but I had done it; I had scored a job in a single day. My theories were right, and I was brimming with pride when I got home that night.

The next Sunday after church, my wife's friend came over to talk to us again. She asked how my job search had gone. I grinned, smugness oozing out of every pore, and told her that I had found a job my first day out. I explained my responsibilities to her, and she asked, "What's the name of the place?"

I told her.

She said, "Oh, that's the job I was telling you about last Sunday." She was genuinely happy I had found that job, glad that Neen and I would be able to buy groceries.

This revelation flushed the smelly pride out of my soul. Of the hundreds of depressed businesses struggling to survive, I stumbled upon the exact place the Lord was trying to tell me about the week before—a business located in a Quonset hut on the backside of a gravel parking lot in the middle of nowhere. The very last place I decided to visit turned out to be the first place I was told about.

What a divine encounter?! If I had listened to her, I could have avoided eight hours of rejection. But that rejection and frustration worked in me like the proverbial dose of salt. I knew without a doubt that God was interested in providing for me.

Amid the apparent chaos of the universe, we see a pattern. In the confusing swirl of people, places and decisions, we happen upon order in a divine encounter. Discovering God's place of protection and provision convinces us that the universe is not a mindless machine, randomly spitting out fortune or misfortune to a hapless humanity. His care for us persuades us that the eyes of the universe are not like the soulless eyes of a shark looking to tear apart its next random victim. Divine encounter is the arbiter between superstition and faith, between belief in good luck and a good God.

Yet Ruth's finding the redeemer's field is only a small corner of the whole picture. A larger issue is discovering why she stayed in the field. Consider what would have happened if she had just passed through the field. How would the story have read if she had just spent a couple of hours picking up some grain and then moved on? Finding the field was essential, but even more important was the fact she was in the field long enough to meet Boaz.

The fields of Boaz are a prophetic image of the New Testament church. They are a blueprint for a Christian community, a community where weak and vulnerable people can find protection and help. These are places that provide an accessible alternative for those seeking refuge from the predators that stalk humanity. The Church is a spiritual entity which is called to release her spirituality in ways that provide an opportunity for folks to meet the Redeemer. The Church has a mandate to create and maintain a place of corporate worship where foreigners, misfits and the less fortunate can participate in a Biblical expression of kindness, provision and goodwill—churches where people like Ruth can find help.

Let's look at a few reasons why Ruth found it easy to stick around long enough to meet Boaz.

BOAZ'S OBEDIENCE TO GLEANING LAWS

First, the Biblical standards for gleaning were being maintained. Apparently, Boaz was a law-abiding Jew, and as such he was not going to allow the corners of the field to be harvested, nor would he have allowed his workers to go back over the field a second time (Lev. 19:9). Both of these laws insured that some grain would be left lying in the fields after they were harvested. This is why gleaning in Boaz's field was more productive than gleaning in the field of someone uncommitted to maintaining the Biblical standards.

Boaz was unique. In a land where everyone was doing what was right in their own eyes, he was doing what was right in the sight of God by scrupulously obeying the laws pertaining to gleaning. Ruth stayed in his field because gleaning was better there.

The fact that gleaning still existed in the environs surrounding Bethlehem tells us that the law was being kept by other farmers, at least in principle though. What I suspect is that over time the size of the corners left for gleaners just got smaller and smaller—token corners, if you will. Farmers probably started sounding like Pharisaical rabbis as they argued for an ever-shrinking definition of corner size. Using creative exegesis and inventive parsing, I'm sure they were able to use the Bible to explain why people gleaning in their fields were not even able to find enough grain for lunch. Downsizing is not just a modern phenomenon.

I'm not sure if that's where our expression "cutting corners" came into existence. I think it may have come from folks who take shortcuts through parking lots to avoid traffic lights. But whatever the origin, cutting corners refers to someone who is not doing things correctly.

Christian communities cut corners whenever we obey the letter of the law rather than the spirit of the law. It's easy to defend all kinds of corner-cutting by saying we don't want to be legalistic. It must have been especially difficult for farmers to leave generous corners for gleaners while the land was beset by those years of famine that drove Elimelech and Naomi into Moab.

Unfortunately, corner-cutting has a negative effect on the weakest and most vulnerable in our midst. It's a possible explanation as to why we don't attract too many Ruths to our business and religious organizations. The size of our corners just keeps getting smaller inch by inch. It's not like one day we just start cutting down the corners of our fields; they slowly recede year after year. Integrity rarely goes away in a moment of time; it goes away bit by bit.

We don't fall into sin; we wade into its scalding bath, giving the skin of our conscience enough time to get acclimated to the change in temperature. Once we're fully immersed, we often encourage others to come on in, exhorting them that it's not that bad.

It would be healthy for us to honestly appraise how easy it is for the truly needy to access our abundance—not just the material poor, but the emotionally and spiritually indigent as well. I love the story about the pastor who dressed like a homeless man and visited his church to see how he would be treated. Like him, we will often discover that the fields we cultivate for the Redeemer are not very friendly or hospitable. Fear and famine are powerful temptations to cut as much of the corner as we legally can. Like any good Pharisee, we want to know just exactly how many square cubits that corner is supposed to be. All of us would do well to imitate the redeemer Boaz and err on the side of big corners; we might be surprised about how many Ruths end up in our fields.

BOAZ'S LANGUAGE

A second possible reason Ruth stayed in Boaz's field was that the language was better. Notice the greetings between Boaz and his foreman. They say things like, *"May the Lord be with you"* and *"May the Lord bless you"* (Ruth 2:4). Boaz's Godly influence had worked its way down into his staff.

We err when we underestimate the power of words. In fact, the Scriptures are packed with exhortations, admonitions and reminders about the power of our words. Let's take a moment to reacquaint ourselves with just a few of these verses, reminding us of both the positive and negative effects words have on our lives. Here are just a few verses to highlight our point.

> *"And I say to you, that every careless word that men shall speak, they shall render account for it in the day of judgment. For by your words you shall be justified, and by your words you shall be condemned"* (Matt. 12:36-37).

> *If you confess with your mouth Jesus as Lord, and believe in your heart that God raised Him from the dead, you shall be saved; for with the*

heart man believes, resulting in righteousness, and with the mouth he confesses, resulting in salvation (Rom. 10:9-10).

Let no unwholesome word proceed from your mouth, but only such a word as is good for edification according to the need of the moment, that it may give grace to those who hear (Eph. 4:29).

And the tongue is a fire, the very world of iniquity; the tongue is set among our members as that which defiles the entire body, and sets on fire the course of our life, and is set on fire by hell (James 3:6).

I think I'll stop quoting verses now because I'm getting way too convicted. Suffice to say that what comes out of our mouths is both an indication of what is going on in our hearts and to some degree a shaper of our environments. When pressure, frustration or anger squeezes my soul, some pretty foul language can leak out of my mouth. Just for the record, and in keeping with the principle of full disclosure, I want you to know that I have cussed at broken lawn mowers, bad drivers and recently I even cussed while preaching a sermon about Satan, but hey, he deserved it!

Boaz knew something about the power of words and blessed his reapers. It's a wise parent that speaks blessing over his kids. Daughters who have fathers who tell them they are beautiful are less likely to seek that affirmation from the creepy kid down the street. It's a wise boss or business owner that speaks blessings of prosperity over her workers or customers. Words are verbal seeds that grow into a mature crop; whether we sow good seed or bad seed is our choice. But make no mistake about it, we will harvest what we plant.

Boaz even used his rightful authority to dictate the kind of language his employees were using in his fields. Note the words of Boaz in his instructions to his reapers concerning their treatment of Ruth: *"And also you shall purposely pull out for her some grain from the bundles and leave it that she may glean, and do not rebuke her"'* (Ruth 2:16). His instruction included not only providing for her but protecting her from the potty-mouthed remarks of the workers. We know that Ruth lived in a dangerous and a godless time in the history of Israel and, therefore, can safely assume the nature of the rebukes that the field workers meted out to gleaners who were getting too close to the harvest was pretty raunchy. I can hear the paid employees lobbing verbal hand grenades to keep the low-life types a respectful distance away from the crops.

In our age, the F-bomb has been dropped so many times that it no longer shocks listeners into the compliance or fear it used to evoke. I feel really sorry for those Marine Corps drill sergeants down there at Camp Lajeune, South Carolina. How can they be expected to get their job done and motivate those fresh recruits now that everyone seems to have learned their patriotic art form? I also feel sorry for those dull-witted comedians who used to make a living by simply throwing some obscenities into their half-soused audience. But most of all I'm sorry that we live in a time when vulgarity has become the norm, in a culture that has been desensitized to virtually every kind of sin. Expletives, racial slurs, crude jokes and crass remarks are an affront to God and should be offensive to His people.

Yet it's also possible to be turned off by someone who lays on the religious lingo. For me, too much religious jargon makes me wary of doing business with someone with his incessant prattle of religious catch phrases. Even worse is someone who cranks up the religious talk only after he discovers I'm a pastor. I'm perplexed by why folks would be so naïve to believe that any thinking believer would be more likely to buy the car he's selling or hire him because he punctuates every other sentence with "Praise the Lord" or "Hallelujah."

Unfortunately, most of us can probably tell a story of being jilted by folks who try to cover up shoddy workmanship and less than ethical practices with a constant stream of pseudo-spiritual platitudes. Most of us have learned the hard way that the fish in the phonebook ad is not a guarantee that the product or service is first-rate. It's why I need to remind myself on a regular basis that, if I'm going to talk the talk, I need to walk the walk.

BOAZ'S HOSPITALITY

Thirdly, I think Ruth stayed around long enough to meet Boaz because she was offered some hospitality. She was allowed to rest in the shade of the shelter. This may seem like a small thing, but laboring in the equatorial sun is exhausting. Unless you have been near the equator, it's difficult to describe just how intense the sun can be there. It can give you a blistering sunburn through a white T-shirt. By eight in the morning, the sun and temperatures can be too intense to sit on the beach. If you've never experienced the sun at these latitudes, ask people who have been there, and they will tell you just how important a little shade can be.

The shelter Ruth was sitting in on the redeemer's property is a prophetic picture of what one facet of church life ought to be like. Churches should offer a place where weary laborers find a moment to regain their strength, even take a little siesta during the heat of the day. It's the kind of shelter and shade the psalmist was talking about when he said, *"He who dwells in the shelter of the Most High will abide in the shadow of the Almighty"* (Ps. 91:1). His shadow was and is a good place to rest, the right place to rest.

I don't like getting yelled at. I think it's one of the reasons I'm nervous about visiting churches I'm not familiar with when I'm out of town. Sometimes, I just want some shade. I have a theory about people who go to churches where they get yelled at every meeting—I think they do so because they feel guilty. If your religion is based on keeping some sort of law or set of rules, then you're never going to measure up to the standard. So it would seem only proper to have a preacher yell at you at least once a week. After all, we should be chastised for not praying enough, giving enough, witnessing enough or attending enough. We take the punishment because we know we're guilty. If your religious boss is yelling at you all the time, if you take it because you know you deserve to be screamed at, it's time to find a new religion.

I'm reminded of Jennifer who was a recovering crack addict. She often slept during our church services. (Insomniacs just have to listen to a few minutes of my preaching to get healed.) She felt a bit guilty about this and confessed to one of our elders that the sleep she got during church was often the most refreshing she got all week. Our elder, who knows something about the need for shade, did not scold or rebuke her. He told her to sleep all she wanted. Jennifer died not too long afterwards. I'm glad she got some rest before she passed away.

BOAZ'S PROTECTION

Finally, Boaz's field was a relatively safe place. Two times in the book of Ruth, there is reference to sexual assault. Boaz tells her that he instructed the servants not to touch her (2:9). Naomi also tells Ruth that working in Boaz's field is a good thing *"so others don't fall on [her] in another field"* (2:22).

Israel during this age was ruled by the whims and consciences of the individual. Rape and sexual molestation must have been common crimes. It was not a safe place for a gal like Ruth who did not have older brothers or a husband to protect her.

In America, we take for granted that our wives and daughters can get on a train or bus and not be molested or groped. But in many other places in the world, this is not the case. In India for example, there are separate trains for men and women. This is because men will simply take their liberties with any women pressed up against them on a crowded train.

Ruth was living in a place not much different than parts of Africa today which are supposedly under the protection of United Nations troops. In these places, women are brutally raped, and the rapists have immunity from prosecution in these lawless regions. These are not places where people like Ruth would want to stay.

One of the primary responsibilities of Christian leaders is making sure church is a safe place. If the Redeemer has asked you to look after one of His fields, then you are responsible for upholding His values and mandates. Sexual predators, religious bullies, anyone and everyone who is not safe must be corrected or run off the property. I am amazed that many Christian leaders seem more concerned about protecting the perceived rights of a dangerous person than protecting the dignity and well-being of frail believers. I'm talking about the older guy who lurks near the exits waiting to hug all the young girls. I'm talking about the young guy who surfs local youth groups looking for wounded and desperate girls to seduce. I'm thinking about that "prophetess" who furtively whispers fearful prophecies to earnest folks coming to the altar for personal ministry.

Ruth stays in Boaz's field long enough to meet him. She didn't know

Boaz, but his fields introduced her to his way of life and his values. The people overseeing his land upheld his values and priorities by providing safe and hospitable places where his abundance could be accessed by the weakest and most vulnerable. We have any number of excellent opportunities to create homes, businesses and churches that reflect the Redeemer's value system—opportunities for His people to not only speak about Him, but to do things that accurately reflect who He is. Our houses and properties should be the right places where the Ruths of the world will stay long enough to meet the Redeemer and find rest.

CHAPTER 8
Nap Time

"'Thus she came and has remained from the morning until now; she has been sitting in the house for a little while'" (RUTH 2:7).

Rest is a four-letter word. Like other four-letter words, it describes something that good Christians aren't supposed to talk about in polite company. To some degree, most of us have come to believe that rest (oops, I said it again) is obscene or dirty. It's something we don't readily admit to doing. We all like to do it, but we never admit to doing it very often. If we do get caught doing it, we make up excuses why we're doing it. We explain how long it's been since we last had any, how much stress we've been under or that we've been a little under the weather lately. Busyness, hard work, labor, these are wholesome words, words that good Christians use.

Have you ever been taking a nap when someone pops in on you? What do you say when your blurred vision, pillow tattoo and groggy countenance make it obvious you've been in the arms of Morpheus? In my stupor, I usually seek absolution by reciting the prescribed liturgy of excuses and justifications. Under no circumstance do good religious people like us ever offer no explanation for having rested our eyes for a few minutes. We are busy worker bees!

The image of Ruth at rest is a prophetic image of the Bride of Christ at rest both spiritually and naturally. The house she is resting in is undoubtedly little more than a roughly constructed and hastily thrown together brush arbor shelter. Palm fronds spread over some branches would have created a patch of shade, a rustic escape from the baking sun. This image of Ruth sitting down for a little while can serve as a powerful prophetic reminder of the true nature of salvation and the essential need for us to regulate the number of hours we work and serve. Unending commitments, constant availability, the frenzied accumulation of wealth, parishioners, team members and equity leave us too exhausted to enjoy the embrace of Him who said, *"'Come unto Me all of you who are weary and heavy-laden, and I will give you rest'"* (Matt. 11:28).

THE GIFT

Boaz the redeemer first put his eyes on his bride while she was sitting down, resting in the shade of that simple shelter. This is an endearing prophetic picture of the New Covenant—the Covenant which is appropriated only when we abandon our attempts to be justified by our works and rest in the shelter and shade of His completed work on the Cross. When Paul wrote, *"For by grace you have been saved through faith, and that not of yourselves, it is the gift of God; not as a result of works, that no one should boast"* (Eph. 2:8-9), he was underscoring both the essential aspect of faith and the inability of works of any kind to secure the favor of God. The idea of works earning, maintaining or retaining the gift of salvation is inconsistent with Biblical revelation. Labor exchanged for compensation is a job. A gift you have to pay for, or pay to keep, is no gift at all.

Don't you love all those e-mails in your inbox telling you about the contest or lottery you just won? Why just today I won £2,000,000.00! All I have to do is call a very nice gentleman in the United Kingdom named Mr. O'Brien to claim my prize. Even now he is probably sipping tea in his tweed jacket, anxiously waiting for me to ring him on the phone and give him my credit card number so he can send me the check. Unlike all those pounds Mr. O'Brien says I've won, salvation is a genuine gift. You can't give the Redeemer your credit card number or promise to put in lots of extra hours to make sure He doesn't take it away.

Don't you love those gifts that people give us and then take back when they discover we're not using them the way they expected? Family members seem really good at giving those kinds of gifts. "Well, if you're not going to use it, I'll take it back" is evidence that your not-so-well-meaning family member was attempting to extract something from you. It might be wrapped in a box, but it's tethered by strings that lead all the way back to the expectations buried in the soul of the giver. When these expectations are unmet, the strings begin to tug and the cloaking devise that disguised the thing as a gift is switched off. Dozens of Trojans scurry out of cash-stuffed envelopes in an attempt to take over our lives.

Don't you love those favors people do for us that are dressed up as gifts? The quid pro quo of human economies and relationships has great difficulty grasping the absolute nature of Father God's benevolence. God is Love (1 John 4:8); therefore, His gift cannot be exchanged for anything we have to offer. We have corporately confused God the Father with the godfather. The puffy-cheeked Don whose gifts and favors had to be returned with interest bears no resemblance to God the Father who gave His Son without expectation or condition to humanity. Somehow, our psyches have been infiltrated with the very human expectation that favors must be returned. Jesus' death on the Cross was not meant to shame or guilt me into a life of service or sacrifice.

Gift-giving is a risky business. Gifts can go unused or misused, can be re-gifted, re-sold, exchanged, thrown away or returned. Redemption was and always will be a risky business. Unrequited love is heartbreaking for mankind and God, yet without the risk, there is no real love. Without this risk, we are left with the same old human condition of legal and social contracts, met and unmet expectations and the never-ending trading of time, skill, energy, possession and favors for the things we need or want.

Boaz was not interested in Ruth for her ability to harvest barley or wheat. He was looking for a lover not a laborer. Ruth could not purchase her redemption with the few mouthfuls of grain her back-breaking labor rewarded her with gleaning in his fields. It's a bit naïve that we have often acted like we could somehow purchase or maintain our redemption with the insignificant produce of a lifetime of labor in the earth that God created. Later, we will learn how she gets the harvest, but suffice it to say for now, she doesn't get it by working. In fact, she begins to receive it while at rest.

THE SABBATH

The believer's rest is not the 24 hours from Friday evening to Saturday night. The believer's rest is the 24/7 freedom from religious duty and activity. Religious activity can be defined as the futile attempt to satisfy, by human effort, the requirements of a Holy God. He who dwells in *"unapproachable light"* is not placated by our personal religious industry (1 Tim. 6:16). There is nothing we can do that will add or subtract from our salvation. The work is complete. *"It is finished"'* (John 19:30). This is the only Sabbath we must keep.

The practical prophetical application of this image lies in discovering a pace of everyday life that allows us to enjoy the embrace of the Lover of our souls while fulfilling our God-given responsibilities. For many believers, this rest seems more elusive to attain than spiritual rest. Being adequately rested in body and soul are essential if we are going to live lives that glorify God for more than a brief season.

The secular madrasas we attend cut deep ruts in our souls. We memorize the mantras of the Ayatollahs who preach the religion of finance. The pursuit of prestige, financial security and external validation is pile-driven into our psyches by the constant pounding of solicitations and social expectation. The promises of financial glory, the voices of the 40 virgins of success, lure us down the suicidal path. They entice us to blow ourselves up in pursuit of their imaginary pleasures. Marriages explode, children get blasted, and ministries go up in mushroom clouds. Undaunted, a seemingly endless line of young zealots stand ready to be sent forth to replace the martyrs of success.

SATAN'S TACTIC

The enemy is not content to just detain his captives; he also tortures them. Noses are held against the grindstone until virtually all creativity, levity and abiding spirituality are ground away by the abrasion of unregulated consumerism and ego. The black hood of external validation has been pulled over our heads. We are bound and gagged while our perverted consciences lash us with counterfeit guilt. "Back to work you dogs," Pharaoh's burly taskmaster cracks the whip, the alarm sounds, the cell phone rings, the Blackberry buzzes. Starved and bloody, we take a puff of the hash grown on Wall Street and stagger back to our self-imposed bondage.

The enemy's goal in all of this is to keep God's children so busy making bricks that they won't have the time or energy to make babies. Ever notice that when we attempt to get off to the wilderness for a few days with the Lord, the Pharaohs in our lives get angry? Our enemy knows that undistracted worship will release a power that he cannot suppress, that waiting on the Lord really does renew our strength (Is. 40:31). His objective is to keep us away from the One who is the sole source of renewal and spiritual power—the power that will break his grip on God's people. The words of the ancient king of Egypt read like they were written just yesterday:

> But the king of Egypt said to them, "Moses and Aaron, why do you draw the people away from their work? Get back to your labors!" Again Pharaoh said, "Look, the people of the land are now many, and you would have them cease from their labors!" So the same day Pharaoh commanded the taskmasters over the people and their foremen, saying, "You are no longer to give the people straw to make brick as previously; let them go and gather straw for themselves. But the quota of bricks which they were making previously, you shall impose on them; you are not to reduce any of it. Because they are lazy, therefore they cry out, 'Let us go and sacrifice to our God.' Let the labor be heavier on the men, and let them work at it that they may pay no attention to false words." So . . . the people scattered through all the land of Egypt to gather stubble for straw . . . . But he said, "You are lazy, very lazy; therefore you say, 'Let us go and sacrifice to the Lord'" (Ex. 5:4-17).

I would be willing to bet a whole pile of money that the Jewish midwives were not very busy nine months after this edict was enacted. Even the powerful and God-given desire to make love can be snuffed out by enough backbreaking labor during the day. Sleepless nights stubble-hunting in Egypt don't do much for the kind of romance that leads to reproduction. The sting of fresh lacerations cut by the taskmaster's whip will extinguish the normal desire to be touched by our lover. The labor demanded by the enemy will quickly turn the marriage bed into a place where the only thing going on is sleep. I know I've spent more than enough time gathering stubble while the Lord waited for me to come home.

Ruth was not lazy. Lazy people don't do manual labor under the blistering sun on an empty or near empty stomach. This is a girl who knew how to work. Her back must have ached terribly from bending over so much. But like all of us, she needed to rest. Without rest, the body revolts. There are short-term issues like heatstroke, which Ruth was avoiding. There are also long-term consequences like mental illness and hypertension that afflict us when we don't enjoy the God-given gift of rest. Herein lies both the prophetic and practical significance in this account.

I'm reminded of something I recently learned about racecar engines. Most racecar engines are rebuilt after every race. Formula One and NASCAR engines are run at such a high RPM, that the engines are worn out after a single race. This seems a fitting picture of how many of us have lived our lives. We go as fast as we can for a few hours, and then we go back to the shop and pray to have our engines and transmissions rebuilt. Our spiritual countryside is littered with the rusting bodies of folks who red-lined their engines until they blew up—good folks who wanted to take the checkered flag for Jesus. These are sincere believers who splashed coffee or soda in their tanks at every pit stop but found out too late that the race would last much longer than their engines. They answered the phone on their day off and caught up on e-mail during their vacation until their health or homes threw a rod or seized up.

I believe in Sabbath-keeping for the purpose of emotional, spiritual and physical health. Not working is an act of faith, both in the spiritual and in the natural. We feel nervous when we take a day off. We worry about not finishing a report on time or the hay getting spoiled. We furtively check e-mails early in the morning while the rest of the family is still sleeping in on vacation. I've seen you in the hotel lobby. Don't lie to me; you work all the time. We find it difficult to trust Him with even one day of the long work week.

Rest that refreshes our spirits, brings renewal to our souls or restores passion and energy to our pursuit of the Lord is different than just "doing nothing." I wish I had a dollar for every game of solitaire I've ever played on a computer. That kind of idleness does so little to help me feel rejuvenated. There is a rest that I experienced, and am hoping to learn to enter into more frequently, that actually sharpens my spiritual acuity. It doesn't leave me feeling groggy and dull. It's a rest that takes place in His presence.

When we boil it down, this is the message and prophetic hope of the entire book of Ruth. Redemption wasn't found frantically picking up the harvest; it came from underneath the blankets. Obed wasn't discovered underneath a pile of grain. He was conceived in the holy union of his mother and father. How we enter this rest is as different and unique as we are. There is no formula, no three-step plan that fits everyone. Discover this gift with your Redeemer.

CHAPTER 9
No Trespassing

*"Then Boaz said to Ruth, 'Listen carefully, my daughter. Do not go to glean
in another field; furthermore, do not go on from this one, but stay here
with my maids. Let your eyes be on the field which they reap, and go after them.
Indeed, I have commanded the servants not to touch you'"* (RUTH 2:8-9).

The grandparents' well-meaning counsel grew increasingly moot as the death total climbed steadily during the day and evening of April 16, 2007. Just eight months before, in the summer of 2006, they had scolded his mom and dad. They accused them of being delinquent, flippant and otherwise just plain lousy parents. They couldn't understand how the parents, the children they had raised, could have allowed their grandson to enroll in a school located in the Third World. To them it was unconscionable for their own children to promote the enrollment of their grandson in a place that would expose him to so many dangers.

After researching the internet and sighting news stories about violent crime and brutal kidnappings that were common in that country, the grandparents pleaded with their children to make their son go to a college or university in the United States where he would be safe. They suggested a university close to home where some of his friends were enrolled. They suggested Virginia Tech.

On that April day, their grandson was safe inside his foreign dormitory when CNN broke the news from back home. He and a few of his American classmates clustered around an old TV to follow the reports streaming from the familiar campus. They watched network news anchors lean into the unusually cold spring wind that blew unceasingly those first few days of the tragedy—reporting in detail how 32 students and faculty were murdered in the benign countryside of southwestern Virginia. The tragedy in Blacksburg, they soon learned, had become the largest mass shooting in the history of American education. With the illusion of safety shattered, parents and grandparents everywhere were nervous; nowhere seemed safe anymore.

Ruth was enrolled in a dangerous place, and Boaz knew it. His relationship with her began with his playing the role of guardian. I'm sure his voice grew firm and fatherly as he spoke to her about not straying from the safety of his fields. *"Listen carefully my daughter"* sounds like something I would say to my girls when I'm trying to impress upon them the importance or perils of a situation. My girls usually say, "Dad, we know," with the typical sigh all young adults sigh when their dads remind them of things they already know. But his words got Ruth's full attention, and she was overwhelmed with gratitude for his loving offer of protection. No doubt, she also understood the danger of the place she was living in.

These words of Boaz to Ruth are a prophetic reminder that our boundaries are a gift from our Redeemer in the same way Ruth's boundaries were a gift from Boaz. Our Redeemer wants us to know where His property lines are so we can be safe. He puts up fences and fine tunes our consciences so we can learn how to live inside the shelter of His protective umbrella. When we are in His fields, we are completely insulated from becoming the victims of anything or anyone He has not permitted onto His property. The expression—"The safest place you can be is in the center of God's will"—is a bit hackneyed but true. Most of my troubles usually start when I climb the fence and start poking around the neighboring fields—those times when I have crossed the boundaries He has erected for my protection and have ignored His admonition not to venture off His property.

As we explore the new land and new Kingdom we have been brought into, we will invariably get near the Redeemer's property lines. Sometimes, we get distracted and innocently walk over the border. On other occasions, our curiosity gets the best of us, and we sneak off His property for a look at what is on the other side of the fence. Sometimes, we even have the audacity to think we can wander around in other fields without consequences.

All of this is normal. No one figures out where all the boundaries are on the first day in the Promised Land, and learning how to correctly interpret the various demarcations of His boundaries takes maturity and practice. This is why the writer of Hebrews wrote: *"But solid food is for the mature, who because of practice have their senses trained to discern good and evil"* (5:14). There are several common ways the Redeemer communicates His boundaries to us.

SIGNS

Clear boundaries common to all believers are spelled out in the plain meaning of the Scriptures. Worshiping another god, taking things that don't belong to you and having sex with someone you're not married to are such boundaries. If you approach the Scriptures with a mind to reason away the moral standards that Christians have observed for 2,000 years, that's your choice. Be advised, however, that once we begin to edit the words of the Bible to fit into the margins we think they need to fit into, we'll face the consequences. I find it maddening that the same folks who usually claim to be seeking the real Jesus are often the first to reject His real authority when it comes to lifestyle.

Crossing these clearly-marked property lines of the Redeemer's land will always cause us far more trouble than the temporary thrill or pleasure of sneaking off the farm for a wild weekend. These ill-conceived forays usually end with believers calling the Redeemer in the middle of the night to come bail them out of the jails they have been thrown into. Or they eventually conclude with the runaway wandering back onto the property like the starving, half-naked prodigal son the Gospel of Luke describes.

Even more disconcerting are the forays that squander the better part of a lifetime. What begins as a lost weekend ends as a lifetime of self-imposed exile from the Kingdom of God—gifted children of God with unlimited potential who just seem to wander off one day. These folks put me in mind of the guy who said he was going to the corner store to fetch a gallon of milk and his family never saw him again. It's heartrending when we consider what could have been if only these gifted believers would have just stayed on the property.

Ruth did not have the access to the Bible like we do. Her knowledge of the God of Abraham, Isaac and Jacob would have been limited to the stories she heard through her husband and in-laws, yet she obeyed some basic instruction. We would do well to follow her example by honoring the clearly marked ethical and moral boundaries that are taught in Scripture. Tampering with the text and the clear meaning of Scripture is about as smart as taking down a stop sign. The fool who takes it down gets to hang the souvenir on his wall while someone else hangs a wreath on a lonely grave. One generation takes down the signs, and the next one gets T-boned by the enemy's 18-wheeler.

Why couldn't they just be like Ruth—and be grateful for the protection?

LIFEGUARDS

At particularly dangerous places, the Redeemer usually assigns some of His workers to tell us when we're getting close to someone else's turf. Funny how often we get angry with the workers who warn us. Disdain for authority is so ingrained in our corrupted human nature that we naturally want to do just the opposite of what someone tells us to do, even when it is for our own good. I have so much rebellion in me that I actually have become miffed at lifeguards at the beach when they had the audacity to blow their whistles and wave me in when I had swam an unsafe distance from shore. I reluctantly obeyed, but in my mind I thought, *Who do those white-nosed, tanned hard bodies think they are any way? If I want to get pulled out to sea by a rip current, that's my business, and I don't need no college-aged clown blowing his *∧&% whistle at me.*

Now, read the verse at the start of this chapter out loud and in an authoritarian tone of voice. Yes, stop what you're doing and right now say this aloud in your best male authority figure imitation: *"Listen carefully, my daughter. Do not go to glean in the field of another."* That was pathetic. Try that again, and this time without rolling your eyes.

Can you hear the Father's voice and feel His passion in these words? Or did you get miffed that I told you to read the verse in a male voice of authority and then criticized your first attempt? I'm sorry, maybe you wouldn't have been offended if I would have asked you to read rather than tell you to read. Or maybe, I should have used my sugary pastor tone of voice to gently coax you into reading out loud. Maybe so, but isn't it interesting that most of us initially recoil from being told what to do, even when the person telling us what to do is right?

Apparently, Ruth had a different attitude toward her God-given protective authority; she obeyed his command without any negative attitude. It's unlikely she rolled her eyes or called a girlfriend to vent her anger and frustration about how the bossy redeemer told her where she should work and where not to go. Ruth, it seems, had a realistic understanding of the very real dangers lurking just over the border as well as the blessings of staying in the field. She didn't get miffed or offended that the old rich guy told her what to do, and it probably saved her life.

LIGHTS

Occasionally, boundaries are lit up and marked by supernatural events that get our attention, steer us away from danger and start us in the right direction. This is how the Apostle Paul was steered out of Asia by the Spirit and then directed by a vision to go to Macedonia (Acts 16:6-10). Supernatural events are a normal part of every believer's life; whether it's an answered prayer, angelic visitation, it's all divine intervention.

Many of us have experienced these supernatural events, or natural events with clearly supernatural implications, that were used by the Lord to clearly lead us. However, this is not God's only way of leading us, so it's not appropriate for us to view these experiences as evidence of a higher level of spirituality. Having an angel stand in front of the stop sign does not make the would-be-vandal more spiritual than the one who read the eighth commandment and decided to obey it.

With that said, I confess I have had the Lord lead me in some supernatural and dynamic ways. But this kind of leading was not always a byproduct of intimacy with Him. In fact, when I look back on when these events occurred, I realize He granted these unusual occurrences to startle me into paying closer attention when my soul was distracted. It's similar to how my teachers in middle school used to chide me because I daydreamed so much in class. They would do their best imitation of the ground controllers in Houston and say, "Earth to Jeff. Earth to Jeff, come in, Jeff." They did this because I was staring out the window, lost in the outer space of my imagination. Now, my Redeemer gets my attention the same way some times, except

He says, "Heaven to Jeff. Heaven to Jeff, come in, Jeff." The blast of heaven's air horn startles me back from orbit. That's me and many of us, looking for the lights to flash and the mechanical arms to flail about while our angel yells, "Danger, Will Robinson, danger."

I'm thankful for the lights and noise that get my attention like those rumble strips on the edge of the highway. Weaving from one shoulder of the road to the other is not the wisest way to navigate to our destinies. Ruth, it seems, didn't need all the lights and supernatural events. She simply heeded the voice of her redeemer. She drove in the center of God's lane for her life and enjoyed the peace and quiet of life without all the drama of warning lights, rumble strips and sirens.

DESENSITIZATION

It sounds quite old fashioned to talk about the human conscience today. In our age, the idea of a conscience seems about as relevant as Jiminy Cricket sitting on Pinocchio's wooden shoulder. Nonetheless, our consciences are still God's way of alerting us that we are approaching one of the many guardrails He has put up for our safety.

The conscience is meant to produce enough pain that we change direction. It is meant to sting us when we are in danger of crossing a line. It's similar to the invisible fencing that is so popular with suburban dog owners these days. The dog is equipped with a pain producing collar that tingles with electricity when the pet approaches the buried barrier in the lawn. The closer the pet gets to the boundary, the more intense the pain. These devises are a very effective and unobtrusive way of keeping little Rover out of the neighbor's garden. Unfortunately, the human conscience is rarely as effective as these invisible barriers. Man, it seems, is not as smart as his best friend.

Humanity has figured out how to disable the antiquated security system of conscience. We have discovered that if we run through the barrier fast enough, it only stings for a little while. We're proficient at stuffing arguments and justifications under our collars so we can walk off the property without feeling hardly a thing. Some of us have even learned how to take the batteries out of our collars. Why we're so clever and smart that we can go to the very places He has warned us about and still come up with creative Scriptural explanations and philosophic arguments as to why it's not really unsafe to be in the neighbor's garden. Then, the neighbor shoots us.

The Apostle Paul used a couple of metaphors to illustrate the phenomenon of a desensitized conscience, a soul that no longer feels the painful sting of violation. In Ephesians 4:19, he describes non-Christians as having become callused—*"And they, having become callous, have given themselves over to sensuality, for the practice of every kind of impurity with greediness."*

In the agrarian culture of Paul's day, this metaphor would have been well understood. Most of the members of the early church would have had hands covered by calluses. Theirs were the hands of slaves, day laborers and moms, who wielded shovels, hoes and scrubbing stones. A callus is thick skin; it gives us the ability to handle things that would otherwise hurt us. It develops slowly to protect a part of our body that is regularly subject to friction and prevents us from getting painful blisters. Unfortunately, the skin of the soul can also thicken with the repetitive friction caused by sinful behaviors. In this way, humanity develops the increased ability to ignore the pain of a violated conscience.

I watched an interview on public TV with a Polish farmer who owned land that abutted a Nazi concentration camp during World War II. Before his death, he gave an interview in which he described his experience of farming in such an awful place. He said that at first he had great difficulty working his land closest to the camp because he was traumatized by the screams of the inmates on the other side of the fence. His horse-drawn implements were quiet; they didn't drown out the sound the way diesel or gasoline motors would, so he could clearly hear the terror occurring nearby. Yet, because it was essential for him to continue working those fields to provide for his family, he had no choice but to keep returning there.

With a shrug of his shoulders and a pursing of his lips, he admitted that, over time, it got progressively easier for him to be in those fields. After a while, he said he just stopped noticing the cries and shrieks of victims inside the camp. How amazing to realize that the moans and howls of human suffering could eventually become like the ticking of the clock on the mantel piece, or the sounds of the road near the house—sounds we don't notice unless someone says something about them. That is a thick callus.

The second Pauline metaphor describes the rapid desensitization of the soul. In 1 Timothy 4:2, he wrote, *"by means of the hypocrisy of liars seared in their own conscience as with a branding iron."* In an age when one-third of the population was slave, this metaphor also would have been readily understood. Slaves were routinely branded like cattle with the initials or emblems of their owners. Branding is the burning of flesh with a superheated metallic object. Intense pain fades after several days, and the wound will eventually be covered by a permanent scar. The scar is flesh where the nerve endings have been burned away and normal metabolic function has ceased.

Paul's graphic metaphor infers that certain sinful beliefs and practices can quickly interfere with mankind's God-given ability to feel pain when our consciences are violated. It's safe to infer that Ruth's conscience had not become desensitized, that she was able to retain her God-given ability to discern right from wrong.

PROPER PITCH

The conscience is a temperamental instrument. Sometimes, we feel its sting when we shouldn't, and other times, we feel nothing when we should. This is why our consciences are not always a reliable way to discern our Redeemer's boundaries. Our consciences need to be brought into harmony with the other boundary markers of the written Word, Godly counsel and supernatural leading.

Before the fall, this was not a problem. In the age of innocence, mankind's yet un-violated conscience was in perfect tune with God's will. Once violated, however, humanity's conscience began to send inconsistent and often inaccurate messages to the human soul.

The disobedience of the first couple brought dissonance to their beings, and so their now un-tuned consciences provoked them to cower in the bushes and feel the sensation of shame for the first time. Ever since, all our consciences have needed maintenance; they require regular retuning and recalibration.

Like the strings on a guitar or piano, our consciences need just the right amount of tension on them if they are going to produce the right sound. If the string is too tightly wound, the note will be sharp. If the string is too loose, the note will be flat. Part of any musician's training includes learning to properly tune her instrument; why even drummers can learn to adjust the tension on their drums so they will sound better.

Religion has the tendency to wind our consciences too tightly. You might know someone who is wound up too tightly on religion. Sometimes, I'm wound up too tightly, my conscience sharply buzzing with the slightest provocation. Religious people want everyone else to tune to their consciences. They can't tolerate the dissonant sounds they hear when they are in proximity to people who have less tension in their consciences. They are usually very certain their strings have the righteous amount of tension on them. Eventually, they start their own little orchestra or band where everyone plays sharp notes.

The early church had to sort out these different notes in the body. Folks who came to Christ from strict Judaism wanted the gentiles to get in tune with their historic beliefs. However, the Holy Spirit wanted believers to get in tune with Him.

If you keep too much tension on your conscience long enough, something eventually breaks. This is why so many very religious people end up doing some really bad things. When someone snaps, it seems so sudden, but in reality, the ungodly amount of stress on them was weakening them all along. Tuning our consciences to the pitch of the Word of God by the power of the Holy Spirit will never wind our consciences too tightly.

Our flesh, on the other hand, wants the strings of our consciences to be as loose as possible. It wants the strings of conscience to sag like the ropes on an old clothesline. It wants us to tune our consciences to the flat pitch of the world so we can be in harmony with our ungodly culture. It too finds dissonance unpalatable and is amenable to being tuned as loosely as possible. In fact, one time my flesh brought forth a very interesting proposal. It suggested that we get rid of the strings altogether. It argued eloquently that the strings were simply an old-fashioned and unnecessary encumbrance, interfering with my creative abilities. That conscience was an old law that needed to be taken off the books. It was brought to the floor for a vote by my soul, but the Holy Spirit vetoed the idea.

Ruth, on the other hand, didn't seem to have this pitch problem. She kept in tune with her commitment of loyalty and service to Naomi, perhaps predisposing her to obey Boaz's command. She is a powerful example of how regular believers can receive the Redeemer's extraordinary protection and provision by simply staying in the place He has told them to be.

NO GOING BACK

Maybe you're wandering around the edges of the Redeemer's property today, contemplating a visit back to the old neighborhood. It is possible you have been walking as close to the edge as you can without actually crossing the line. At these times, our minds cleverly delete all the negatives and paste up a photo-shopped, air-brushed memory of the good old days. Maybe you're already halfway over the fence or all the way over. Before you get all the way over the fence or any further from His fields, why don't you take a moment and let the Spirit of God impress upon you the importance of staying on the Redeemer's property. You're in a more dangerous place than you probably realize, and now I am begging you to pay attention in the sweetest way I know how.

Please, pretty please, understand, you can't go back to your old neighborhood. Believers are like gang members who have left their old gang. Once you leave, you become a marked man or woman. Your old gang is now your worst enemy. If they catch you, they are going to punish you for your desertion. This is one of the reasons believers are so miserable when they backslide. The enemy has them back on his turf and is going to make an example of them to make sure the other members see the consequences of desertion. We find ourselves in a once familiar part of town we have no business being in, facing an enemy that takes great pleasure in beating us bloody and dragging our bodies through the street. And because we are trespassing on his territory, he can work us over with impunity.

The children of Israel talked of going back to their old neighborhood, Egypt. Their minds conveniently deleted the seven-day work weeks, infanticide of their sons and subservience to the Egyptians. They only remembered the good food and good times, and so they pined for the good old days which they had forgotten were actually not very good.

Nevertheless, the idea of going back had become a very appealing alternative to many of them. Life in the desert under the leadership of Moses was not perfect. So, like in all social organizations, a group opposed to the existing leadership emerged with its campaign to replace the current leadership and lead the nation in a "new direction." The Back-To-Egypt Party was formed; they held a convention and nominated Korah to be their candidate (Num. 16:1). They gathered 250 influential tribal leaders (Num. 16:2). They even got a catchy slogan, "Remember the leeks and onions." Eventually, they kind of fell through the cracks and went away (Num. 16:31). But what would have happened if they would have been successful in their campaign? What would it have looked like if they had won the election, and with Korah at the helm, the nation changed course and went back to Egypt?

I don't think the Back-To-Egypt Party ever considered the kind of reception that would have awaited them if they had returned. Did they really think the Egyptians had forgotten about their lost jewelry, scarred skin, environmental contamination, ruined crops, dead livestock and all the funerals for their firstborn? I'm sure those Egyptians would have *loved* to have seen those Jews back in town. They would have thrown them a big welcome back party, I'm sure.

Silly, isn't it? Did the grumbling Israelites really think they could go back? Were they actually naïve enough to believe that they could ever reintegrate into the land they had left? Actually, I think they were that naïve. I believe this because all too often we Christians think the same things today. We convince ourselves we can return to our old haunts and the gang will just accept us back like nothing happened. We still think it's safe for us to roam into any field we want to. But we are wrong to think this, dead wrong.

Ruth was smart. She read the No Trespassing sign and stayed put. Oh, to be so obedient!

CHAPTER 10
First Date

"And at mealtime Boaz said to her, 'Come here,
that you may eat of the bread and dip your piece of bread in the vinegar.'
So she sat beside the reapers; and he served her roasted grain,
and she ate and was satisfied and had some left" (RUTH 2:14).

My wife paid for our first date. I was so broke that I could not afford to take her out, so she paid for dinner and the movie. All I was able to contribute to the evening was the car I borrowed from another student.

Neen and I have been married for more than 20 years, and I still remember many of the details of that night. We ate Mexican food and went to a movie called *The Iceman* (which may have been the worst movie ever made). I lost my grandfather's watch in the theater. After the movie, I couldn't get the car started and thought I had broken it. Neen quickly noticed I had not placed the car in park. I put the car in park, and it started right up. Funny how such a great relationship started with such a lousy first date.

Whenever we tell this story to our girls, they laugh. Even though they have heard the story dozens of times, they always get quizzical looks on their faces when we tell them how mom paid for the date. They wonder how someone so amazing, so beautiful, so perfect would have wanted to continue in a relationship with a guy who couldn't even pay for his own dinner. I wonder the same thing.

In Ruth's story, Boaz has brought Ruth under his protective wing. If the story ended here, it would have been enough. Finding blessing, the protection and provision of the redeemer, is no small thing. But, of course, the desire for something more stirred inside of Boaz. He had seen Ruth. There was now a face and form to go with the reputation and accounts of Naomi's unique daughter-in-law. Was it her face? Her figure? What was it in Ruth that Boaz noticed, starting these two down the path to marriage? We may never know, but one thing is certain: Boaz took the initiative. Thankfully, we have a verbal snapshot of their first date.

THE SNAPSHOT

The scene unfolds with Boaz traveling into the countryside to inspect the harvest and check in on his laborers. He sees a stranger, discovers who she is and offers his provision and protection.

Later in the day, a meal is prepared and served to the workers. A simple meal is a typical part of the compensation paid to agricultural workers in most ages and places and is still practiced here in America today. In fact, some farms in Idaho only serve egg salad sandwiches, boiled eggs and egg yolk drink to their workers. Glad I don't work there.

Boaz sits down with his employees for some informal conversation. Lunch is ready; people line up or cluster around the bread and vinegar, familiar faces, and undoubtedly the usual banter begins between people who work together—the talk about the weather, gossip about relationships and laughter at their inside jokes, the same kind of social interactions we all have at our jobs.

Off to the side in the background is the foreign gleaner. She is not part of the team. She is working in the field because the law says she can. The owner has no obligation whatsoever to provide anything to a gleaner. She is alone, she doesn't know a soul, and she doesn't have lunch. She is lonely and hungry, and maintaining a respectful distance from the others. And besides, when you're hungry, the last thing you want to do is sit around watching other people eat, like the kid who forgets his lunch and has to sit in the school cafeteria watching all the other kids scarf down lunch. After even a few minutes of that, the greasy sloppy joes and the limp green beans start looking pretty good.

Apparently, the other workers are ambivalent toward Ruth. Like most of us, they are often blind to the needs of others around them. It's lunchtime, time to hang out with friends and enjoy some hard-earned rest afterwards. It's likely that Ruth's ethnicity plays into the lack of hospitality offered by the other maids and workers. Maybe they thought Ruth should go back to Moab and glean there. They may have believed foreigners did not have the right to access the welfare system provided by the Jews and for the Jews. They may have had issue with outsiders taking bread away from hungry locals who could have been gleaning that field.

That's why it must have been a tremendous shock when Boaz asks her to join him for lunch and does so right in front of everyone. Heads pivot with open mouths as Ruth sheepishly creeps into the circle. A sudden silence falls on the crowd. Ruth nervously heads for the meal under the perplexing stares of the locals. Here was something they didn't see in the lunch room every day.

I also like to imagine that, when Boaz called out to Ruth, there was a moment of innocent disbelief. That when he said, *"'Come here,'"* she innocently turned about to see who he was speaking to behind her. It just may be that, when she saw there was no one else he could have been talking to, she put her brown finger on her chest and said, "Are you talking to me?" Her shock is observed by Boaz, so he says "Yeah, you. I'm talking to you." He motions for her to come on over and get some lunch. Unbelievable!

When the Redeemer invites us into lunch, it is a shock. My personal insecurities have often fueled an unhealthy understanding of the Redeemer's love for me as an individual. I can accept that *"God so loved the world"* and know that He loves me because I'm part of the world. Yet, this realization that He wants to do lunch with me, just me, has been more difficult to understand. I certainly have experienced the disbelief I assume Ruth did when her redeemer asked her to eat with him.

At the end of the age, folks who prophesied, performed exorcism and did miracles in the name of Jesus will be sent to hell because He did not know them. This is and should be a frightening reminder of both judgment and the need for personal relationship with Him. But what I find more frightening is the fact that He does know me. He knows my rising up and my sitting down; He scrutinizes my thoughts from afar. The eyes of the Lord roam to and fro in the earth, and nothing is hidden from His sight. This is why it's such a jolt to my being; He knows me and still waves me over to have lunch.

When the Redeemer personally serves us lunch, it's even a greater surprise. I don't get the feeling from the text that Boaz was waiting on all the other employees. It says literally, *"He served her roasted grain."* She alone was eating from his hand. Evidently, someone had kindled a fire, and they were enjoying grain roasted on an open fire. Boaz is like the summer camp's expert marshmallow roaster and cooks up some perfectly toasted grain just for her. Glad the Scriptures give us some of these details of the beginnings of their romance. Wonder what the other workers thought of this special attention the little foreign forager was having lavished upon her by the big guy? I see her accepting his gift, bashfully receiving the first fruits of his harvest. Maybe he was already thinking, "Baby, you ain't seen nothing yet."

THE FORESHADOWING

David knew something about the Redeemer's feeding when he sang about the Shepherd preparing a table for him in the presence of his enemies (Ps. 23). So did his great-grandmother Ruth. It's very unlikely Ruth lived long enough for them to have ever met. But this chosen line of the house of David experienced the provision of God in some unlikely places, places where only God was looking out for them. I wonder if David remembered the stories about his great-grandmother when he was a fugitive and the entire nation was on alert to apprehend him. I wonder if the Son of David thought about the redeemer's gift of roasted grain when the angels came to minister to Him after His temptation in the wilderness.

Gary Chapman has written a book, the very title of which tells us there are five love languages, five ways of expressing how we show and receive love from those around us. In *Five Love Languages*, Chapman identifies these languages as: acts of service, words of encouragement, quality time, gift giving and physical affection. Boaz is able to speak four of the five on the first date. I mean, this guy is good. He serves her lunch, speaks kindly to her, eats lunch with her and pays for her lunch! Physical affection is reserved for after the wedding; nevertheless, Ruth has come to understand the character of her redeemer before she makes herself completely vulnerable to him. She knew things about Boaz before she ventured into the threshing floor that night.

Our initial interactions with the Redeemer are often very similar to Ruth's with Boaz. He reveals His nature and His character to us early on in our relationship. This first revelation of His nature allows us to trust Him in the ever deepening and spiritually romantic relationship He is calling us to.

If we believe that God is not good, then we will always be wary of how close we get to Him. In fact, if we believe that He is dangerous, then we will avoid Him whenever possible. We become like employees who scatter when the angry boss is on the floor, or children who go play outside when their drunken father gets home. Better to fly under the radar than become the object of his anger, wrath or rants. If we think this about God, then we run away when He walks into our gardens.

Without some knowledge of his character, it is unlikely that Ruth would have taken the risk of lying at his feet in the middle of the night. Inevitably, all believers will find themselves in places and predicaments when all the evidence is pointing toward a god who is not good. Naomi's Almighty, in her eyes, had suddenly turned a deaf ear and blind eye toward the sickness, persecution or hardship she and her loved ones faced. Like Naomi, for many of us, trusting God's character in these seasons is exceedingly difficult. It is the essence of faith, the Job-like experience of cursing everyone and everything but the Redeemer.

The snapshot of Boaz's holding out the grain to nervous Ruth is so endearing. His loving eyes gently inviting her closer, holding forth the grain like a child holding out an apple to draw a skittish colt close enough to pet. I'd like to think their hands touched when she took the grain from him—just a second or two of contact longer than was needed for her to receive it, a touch of warm flesh on the hand of the tired, lonely foreign girl. I believe it probably was a touch that she thought about later and, perhaps, dismissed as just her foolish imagination. Maybe it was even a first touch they giggled and teased each other about the rest of their long married lives.

The first time the Lord touches us is similar to this. We were living a life of unbelief or nominal belief and really had no expectation or hope that God was real. Religion was for others; God was an idea; the universe was a bio-mechanical phenomenon that was beautiful and fascinating to be sure but without supernatural supervision and intervention. We saw religions as the fabrication of social engineers who exploited humanity's natural inclination towards superstition to assist in keeping them in power. Then we got touched.

We heard something or saw something that had no natural explanation. A prayer was prayed in fear or desperation, and we thought it got answered. We secretly tried it again. Our cynicism was subtly replaced by a cautious reverence. We stopped mocking the TV preachers the way we used to. We began to wonder, *What if He is who He says He is? What if Jesus really is God?* Yes, God is Love, and coming to know Him is the most sacred of all human experiences. Being drawn into romance with the divine is what humanity was created for.

THE IMAGE

The serving of roasted grain to Ruth by Boaz evokes a number of Scriptural images of Jesus' serving food to the first disciples. He serves the 5,000 by passing the bread and fish to His disciples who in turn serve the multitude. He serves them the bread and the cup of the Passover meal. One meal in particular, the account of the breakfast Jesus cooked on an open fire for His men early one morning along the banks of the Sea of Galilee, stirs a part of my soul that is typically buried beneath layers of activity, concern and preoccupation, insulating me from His touch. It's the story of a hot meal served to cold men.

Peter had initiated the return of the eleven back home from Jerusalem. I'm sure they were a pretty pathetic sight as they tried to pick up where they left off some three years earlier. Back to the boats, nets and fish mongers—the daily grind of familiar faces, and lots of explaining to the hometown crowd who had followed their short spiritual careers with mixed feelings. Sure there were some victories and a few glorious moments, but suddenly the spiritual season came to a mysterious end. They had been with Him after His resurrection, touched Him and eaten with Him and listened to His words after He had come back from the dead. But then He was gone again. What were they supposed to do now? Peter announced that he was going back to work, *"I am going fishing"* (John 21:3), and the rest followed him back to the lake.

Not too long after their return they spent the night fishing and had caught nothing. At dawn Jesus called to them, *"Children, you do not have any fish, do you?"* (John 21:5). He got them to cast their nets on the right side of the boat, and a tremendous catch was hauled in. John 21:9-13 says:

And so when they got out upon the land, they saw a charcoal fire already laid, and fish placed on it, and bread. Jesus said to them, "Bring some of the fish which you have now caught." Simon Peter went up, and drew the net to land, full of large fish, a hundred and fifty-three; and although there were so many, the net was not torn. Jesus said to them, "Come and have breakfast." None of the disciples ventured to question Him, "Who are You?" knowing that it was the Lord. Jesus came and took the bread, and gave them, and the fish likewise.

This account of my Lord's cooking a meal on an open fire in the pre-dawn light speaks to a place embedded deeply in my soul—that nameless expanse in every human soul wanting to be fed. It's the part wanting to be personally invited into relationship—that part of our beings that wants to be weak, wants to be needy, wants to be wanted. It's the part longing for the whole world to shrink into a circle of guys eating around a campfire with Jesus.

Daybreak is often a time when important spiritual things happen. It's the time of day Jacob's wrestling match ends. It's in the predawn light when Jesus goes off to pray by Himself, and it's the time of day when He stands before Pilate and when Mary Magdalene discovers the empty grave. It's also the time of day when Ruth will get her first installment of grain from Boaz.

Throughout the Scriptures, daybreak is used as a metaphor for God's coming blessing. Isaiah looking to the coming Messianic age wrote, *"Arise shine; for your light has come, and the glory of the Lord has risen upon you'"* (60:1). It's the time of day Jesus reconnects with His beleaguered apostles.

In the natural order of things, these hours are also unique. They are the time of day when our body temperature is the coolest. A cooling core temperature is part of the body's natural daily cycle; it's why when we're sick our fevers are the lowest in the morning. It's also the time of day when the desire to sleep is the most intense, ask anyone who works the graveyard shift about how difficult it is to stay awake this time of day. It's why law enforcement agencies raid suspected drug houses during these hours. It's the time of the day when air temperatures are usually the lowest and dew forms on the ground. It's the time of day when the roads are empty and you don't have to stand in line for your coffee. The old quip about it always being darkest before the dawn has some experiential truth in it. It's the time of day Jesus chooses to step back into the lives of the men He had lived with for three years.

He knows when we're not doing well, just like He knew the condition of his men who had staggered back to their old stomping grounds, disillusioned and discouraged. His remedy for their situation was not a half-time pep talk or all-night harangue. What they needed and what they got was His cooking some fish and grilling some bread. No visions of heaven, no fireworks or supernatural revelations. They got breakfast. There is something so calming about this story. The war is over. He has fulfilled His purpose. He has been to the grave and back, and now He is only days away from His ascension and installation as King of Kings and Lord of Lords. He is the Son of Man, the Son of God. Yet, He kneels down to kindle a fire and cooks some breakfast for His hungry friends.

If we had a snapshot of the moment, I assume Peter would be the one closest to the fire. I can see him squatting over the coals as he nearly touches the glowing embers with his palms. He would have been chilled to the bone; surface water temperatures in the Sea of Galilee are in the low 60's (17-18 degrees Celsius) that time of year, and he had just swum to shore. Shivering, draped in soggy wool, drops of water fall off his beard and sizzle into steam, the smell of fresh bread and crispy fish. Lazy smoke rises a few feet, gives up and drifts over the lake to watch wisps of vapor curl and twist in the mirrored lake before vanishing. Some of the bigger fish from their catch are laid out on the coals. Hungry young men crowded around a campfire with the Creator of the Universe; one meal and everything is right in their world again.

Within the hour, Peter is going to have to correctly answer the most important questions he or any other person will ever be asked. The questions all of humanity will be asked. But as important as those questions are, they will have to wait. I suppose Jesus understands that all of us are more likely to give correct answers after we've eaten a good breakfast. Peter passes his retake exam with flying colors; his triple failure on that dark night a few weeks earlier has been erased for eternity.

So when they had finished breakfast, Jesus said to Simon Peter, "Simon, son of John, do you love Me more than these?" He said to Him, "Yes, Lord; You know that I love You." He said to him, "Tend My lambs." He said to him again a second time, "Simon, son of John, do you love Me?" He said to Him, "Yes, Lord; You know that I love You." He said to him, "Shepherd My sheep." He said to him the third time, "Simon, son of John, do you love Me?" Peter was grieved because He said to him the third time, "Do you love Me?" And he said to Him, "Lord, You know all things; You know that I love You." Jesus said to him, "Tend My sheep" (John 21:15-17).

Once Boaz handed that roasted grain to Ruth, things were never going to be the same again. There was a romantic spark that traveled down the redeemer's hand, through some grain and grounded in her soul. In route, that spark ignited the tinder of Ruth's heart. The fact that they were surrounded by sweaty agricultural workers in the heat of the day, eating plain food made no difference to them; for these two that field might as well been a swank bistro on a warm night in Paris. Many great relationships, it seems, start out in less than perfect surroundings. All that matters is that we have heard the Redeemer say, "Come here that you may eat," or "Come and have breakfast." All that matters is that He has asked us to eat with Him.

CHAPTER 11
UFOs

"And at mealtime Boaz said to her,
'Come here, that you may eat . . .'" (RUTH 2:14).

"So they named him Obed.
He is the father of Jesse, the father of David" (RUTH 4:17).

R uth and Boaz are prophetic archetypes of the members of Christ's Body, a diverse community of foreign-born spiritual immigrants. I like to call us members Unloved Foreign Objects (UFOs) of God's love and grace.

Indeed, God's Kingdom is a nation of Ruth-like aliens who are destined to marry into the family line of David and change the course of history. Nonnative sons are both the ancestors of David, King of Israel, and of Christ, King of the Universe. The incarnate God-Man, Christ Jesus, is not the offspring of pure ethnic Jewish blood. He is the direct descendant of two foreign-born women who were converts to Judaism. The ancestors of Christ are an apt picture of the Bride for whom He came and for whom He is returning. She is a multinational, multiethnic, multilingual people from every corner of the globe and family on earth.

AMERICA'S *MOTHER OF EXILES*

In October of 1969, our fourth grade class went on a field trip to the *Statue of Liberty.* We rode the school bus down the New Jersey turnpike, inhaling all the exhilarating sights and smells of places like Newark and Bayonne along the way.

The upper floors of the nearly completed Twin Towers glistened in the bright sky that its sun-capped peaks rose to meet. The blue-steel eyes of freshly recruited twin sentries kept watch over the Manhattan skyline that was still wrapped in an orange blanket of mist and smog—the sulfur shawl that still clings daily to the widowed city's chilly shoulders until her mourning minions have downed their second cup of joe.

When we got to the *Staten Island Ferry*, we dashed on deck, making sure to avoid the few straggling commuters whose dark eyes and pastry-swelled faces scowled at our exuberance from behind their newspapers' shrouds. Some kids were claiming dibs on seats while others of us leaned over the ferry's gunnels to peer into the oily water and watch garbage lap against the hull.

The whistle blew, mooring ropes were cast off, and the ferry carried us over the waters of New York harbor to Liberty Island. I guess field trips to the *Statue of Liberty* are one of the few perks of growing up in New Jersey.

As we got off the ferry, our teacher, Mrs. Zelnick, took command. Looking sharp in her cat-eye glasses and a new bouffant do, she directed the contingent of stay-at-home moms helping chaperone the trip to herd us off the dock and over to the base of the pale green icon. Field trips were supposed to be educational after all, so before we were allowed to climb up into the edifice, we needed to learn something. A smart girl was selected to read the famous poem engraved into its base; meanwhile, my friends and I scuffled around punching each other in the arms and attempted to pull up some good wedgies.

Miss Preppy Goodie Two Shoes began to read aloud; her school-bell voice was clear, and her tone pregnant with disdain for immature and uncultured morons like me who were not paying attention and messing around when we should have been listening. I didn't understand a thing until she slowed the pace of the recitation near the end of the poem for theatric effect. It was then that the poem became alive; it was as if my innermost being was able to suddenly grasp the profound meaning of these words that welcomed emigrants from every nation and land: "Give me your tired, your poor."

The words launched me into deep and profound philosophic musing: *I'm tired and kind of hungry. Wonder when we get to eat lunch?* We had put our lunches in a box that was left on the bus; my mom had written my name in magic marker on the brown paper bag. She had made me a meatloaf sandwich from last night's leftovers. Saliva pooled in my mouth; my insatiable appetite stirred as I visualized the contents of the bag—potato chips, Shop-

Rite grape soda and vanilla wafers. But the stilted voice broke my trance—
"Your huddled masses yearning to breathe free."

A huddle, now there was something I really understood. We always got
into a huddle to draw up the play when we played two-hand touch football
on the street. We drew complicated receiving routes on the chest of the guy
whose back was to the defense: the button hook, the bomb and the always
effective five and out. Some of those offensive schemes are actually being used
in the NFL today. *On three, ready break,* a perfectly synchronized clap of the
hands, and my imaginary pickup team spread across the width of the street.
The lilting whine interrupted my thoughts again—"The wretched refuse of
your teeming shore."

*What the heck is wretched refuse anyway? Maybe that's what we smelled on
the turnpike? Seems like we already have enough garbage floating around the harbor without asking for more. Last time my dad and I went surf fishing down at
Sandy Hook, I found a needle washed up on shore, for some reason he wouldn't let
me keep it. We never kept any of the fish we caught either, wonder why?* I thought.

For a final time, the neat voice descended into my lowly world. But this
time her cadence slowed to almost a dead stop. Though she was short, she
was looking down at us from her pedestal; her eyes brimmed with contempt
as she gazed upon me and the other unwashed Neanderthals floating about
the fringes of the semicircle. She punctuated the poem's final sentence with
exaggerated diction. She was an oratory prodigy, a preteen genius who trans-
posed poetry into a verbal drubbing. Such talent was destined for the major
leagues; HMO's, insurance companies and college admissions departments
would soon be drafting girls like her in the first round. She would someday
go on to take a starting position among the primped matrons of society who
staff the unwelcoming committees of women's clubs and neighborhoods. She
would be one of society's citizen soldiers who guards the harbor of her culture
armed only with a condescending smile cast in her tanned patina.

"I lift my lamp beside the golden door," she said. There was a tear in that
little girl's voice as she read the last line of the poem—nostalgia, regret and
disappointment mingled with the unmistakable tone of resignation. Like her
mother before her, she would have to bravely accept the fact that she was to

grow up in a nation corrupted by the assimilation of those with inferior genetic pedigrees. Undoubtedly, she was mourning the loss of the opportunity, the mental torture of fantasizing about what could have been, if only the giant woman at the door had done a better job of protecting her world from the flotsam that had washed up on these pure shores. Surely, she was thinking that if *Lady Liberty* had been smart like she, she would have used her flame to torch the hovels that had sheltered the grandparents of those who threatened her comfort and offended her budding sensibilities.

But no, she had let down the whole team and foolishly lifted her torch to light up the front door of the pristine nation. If Miss Goodie Two Shoes had been there, things would have been different. She would have used the giant bronze tablet to squash the vermin that were infesting the manicured lawns and flowerbeds of her suburban Eden. Like Eve, America's most famous lady had erred, and every generation since was paying for her mistake.

The torture eventually ended, and we were instructed to walk, not run, over to the line going into the statue itself. We sprinted to the entrance and slipped under the skirts of the *Mother of Exiles* and began climbing single-file up the ladder-like metal stairs that led up to her crown.

Occasionally, the winding vertical column would come to a sudden halt while somewhere above us someone stopped to catch his breath. Eventually, we came to a narrow catwalk that ran parallel to a set of porthole like windows. A security guard granted us only a few seconds to glimpse New York harbor through the small openings in *Lady Liberty's* tiara. We were shooed off the catwalk and started our descent.

Of course, we were too young to truly appreciate the fact we were looking down from the very same statue that many of our grandparents looked up at when they came across the Atlantic not too many years before. Many of my classmates were kids with last names like Debasse, Artiglare, Sodano, Iorio and Chipoletti—all Sicilians whose grandparents still spoke Italian and would have clearly remembered seeing the welcoming torch high above the harbor. We can only imagine how glorious a sight the statue's dull green skin was after their miserable voyage in the steerage of dilapidated ships. For those immigrants, this really was the "golden door," the new world, the land where dreams could come true, the place to start over. They had crossed the waters and entered the land of milk and affordable mortgages.

A NATION OF EMIGRANTS

The Kingdom of God is populated exclusively by foreigners; one's family tree has no bearing on citizenship. Perhaps you have just disembarked the boat and found new life in Christ a few days ago. Your recent arrival does not relegate you to a second-class status in the Kingdom of God. There is no spiritual caste system that relegates the newest arrivals to a corner of the Kingdom furthest away from the throne of God.

First generation Christians are full citizens of the nation, even if you don't know all the language yet or you have shown up to the dock with lots of ideas and baggage that are never going to make it past customs. Your personal relationship with Christ forever identifies you as a citizen of His universal Kingdom. With this citizenship comes all the privileges and responsibilities afforded to every member of the universal Church.

This is not a new idea; the Kingdom of God was and always will be a refuge for foreigners. Old Testament law foreshadowed the New Testament Age with laws prohibiting the mistreatment of aliens and sojourners (Ex. 22:21). Additionally, the people of Israel were enjoined to show love for the alien and stranger among them. This love for the alien was to be a reflection of God's love for the outsider and a reminder of the nation's status as strangers and aliens in the land of Egypt (Deut. 10:18-19). There is nothing new about God's will to embrace all nations and peoples of the earth; it has been on His heart from the first day of creation.

The New Testament is even more explicit about the Church's being a refuge for all peoples regardless of national affiliation or ethnic background. In Ephesians, Paul wrote concerning the segregation of Jews and gentiles. He asserted it was disintegrated by the blood of Christ—*"But now in Christ Jesus you who formerly were far off have been brought near by the blood of Christ. For He Himself is our peace, who made both groups into one, and broke down the barrier of the dividing wall . . ."* (Eph. 2:13-14). The dividing wall Paul referred to was the wall that kept gentiles from moving past the outermost court in the ancient Jewish temple. The court of the gentiles allowed non-Jews to worship God from a distance, but they were never allowed to move any closer.

This masonry wall known as the *Balustrade* or *Soreg* was about four feet high and had numerous openings where Jewish worshipers could pass through to enter the inner courts. At each entrance, there was a sign written in Greek or Latin warning gentiles who ventured past these checkpoints that they were subject to death. Several of these warning signs which were chiseled into stone have been unearthed in archeological digs in Jerusalem. Philo, the ancient historian, recorded that beating with clubs was the method of execution for gentiles trespassing into the part of the temple reserved for Jews. He graphically recorded that trespassers would be dragged back to the court of the gentiles and have their brains split apart with clubs. The wall of separation and segregation was the wall that Christ demolished by His death, burial and resurrection.

The crime of bringing gentiles into the temple was the pretext for assaulting Paul when he returned to Jerusalem and testified of what the Lord was doing among the gentiles (Acts 21:17ff). In an attempt to appease the religious community, Paul was encouraged to have his companions obey the temple's rituals for purification—that included having their hair shaved off. If you have ever been to a military basic training graduation ceremony, you will know how difficult it is to recognize men from one another when they all have had their heads shaved. It's not uncommon for moms to not even recognize their own sons at these ceremonies.

Undoubtedly, this case of mistaken identity was not really a mistake, just an opportunity for a violent and backslidden religious community to release some of their wrong-minded religious zeal. Paul's good faith effort to accommodate the religious community was just one in a series of events that released the church from its unhealthy association with Judaism. Not too many years after this, in 70 A.D., gentile Roman armies would not only enter the temple but completely raze it, fulfilling Jesus' prophecy about the destruction of that temple and the subsequent rebuilding of it with His own Body (John 2:19-22).

It has been nearly 2,000 years since the temple in Jerusalem was replaced by the Body of Christ that lives in every corner of the world. Jesus' Body brought an end to segregation for God's people. Unfettered and unrestricted access to the Holy Place, the very throne of God, is now the birthright of every human being who has been born again. These people of God are a nation of emigrants who have become citizens in the Kingdom of God and are now aliens in the world they live. Their citizenship and national loyalty are now vested in the spiritual country and Kingdom that Christ has established on the earth, a nation without borders, official language or standing army. It's a monarchy where Jesus is King.

Boaz and Ruth, we will discover, are the perfect poster children for our multiethnic spiritual nation. They are both outsiders who become central figures in the ancient nation of Israel and archetypes of the diverse Church of Christ. Their less-than-perfect pedigrees speak to us today to carry on the mission of welcoming folks into our midst who don't look like us.

ILLEGAL IMMIGRATION

Illegal immigration is a hot-button topic for most nations in the world today. The majority of the world's nations are carefully restricting the flow of foreigners allowed to enter their country and become fulltime residents or citizens. Three fears—job loss, cultural dilution and terrorism—are driving the political move to restrict the flow of illegal immigration. These fears are also fueling an increasingly hostile and agitated attitude among angry and disenfranchised residents. While these fears may be valid concerns for secular nations, the people of God must not allow similar fears to ferment into a toxic religious culture that makes it difficult for those who have recently been born again to find a home in the Body of Christ.

No one likes to lose his job. This is a real issue when your family depends on you to pay the bills and put food on the table. However, job loss is not a legitimate fear in God's Kingdom. Defending your job and territory in the Kingdom or your local church is completely contrary to the will of God. Every ministry we participate in is actually under the administration of the Holy Spirit; we should simply be endeavoring to serve at His pleasure.

Additionally, we are mandated to train up others to do our jobs and replace us (2 Tim. 2:2). If we are doing the same job for our entire lives, it can only mean that we have not learned any new skills or developed a legitimate strategy for expansion. Unfortunately, we often become comfortable in a role or position and defend our territory like dogs growling over their food. We bare our teeth to anyone who gets too close to our dish and nip, especially at young pups that have not learned their place. All of Jesus' workers are replaceable, and seniority does not guarantee position.

No one likes to lose his culture. This too is a valid concern for nations that are being overrun by immigrants whose moral values threaten to undermine the principles of freedom and justice that were won by the sacrifices of their founders. Yet, national or ethnic culture is a non-issue in the Kingdom of God. God is not a God who cow-tows to the cultural distinctive of any nation, denomination or people. The fear of losing one's church culture is especially insidious; this fear is twisted like a tourniquet around the Body and cuts it off from the life-giving flow of His Spirit. The status quo is engraved in granite tablets that soon become the headstones of movements and denominations. Culture changes, technology changes, methods change, everything and everyone but God changes and eventually dies. Refusal and resistance to change will eventually choke churches and institutions to death. If newcomers are not finding their way into our churches, the problem lies with us.

No one likes to lose her life. Terrorism is a real concern for the nations of the earth who are increasingly vulnerable to this manipulative violence. Unfortunately, longtime residents of the Kingdom sometimes eye newcomers as potential terrorists to their way of life and their comfortable status quo. Sure, we all deny our prejudices, but our actions and behaviors betray our inner thoughts. This is why we expect newcomers to give up their seats on the bus we call the local church. We expect newcomers to move to a seat up front where we can keep an eye on them while we remain entrenched in our favorite bunker in the back, privately critiquing the sermon and the music. We say we want new people in our congregations but demonstrate that we really don't mean it when we sit with the same folks at church picnics and potluck suppers. Congregations turn into clubs that meet in tree houses where the ladder has long ago been pulled up.

YOUR MOTHER

Not only was Ruth a foreigner, but Boaz himself was only half Jewish. His mother was Rahab, a former prostitute from the Canaanite city of Jericho (Matt. 1:5). She became a traitor to her own nation by hiding the spies that went to Jericho to reconnoiter the city before Israel attacked it. In an attempt to disguise their activities, the two spies went to a place where it was not unusual to see different men at all hours of the day and night. A house of prostitution was one of the few places where the appearance of strangers would not arouse the curiosity of the neighbors.

Their ruse ultimately failed, and Rahab ended up hiding them under a pile of flax and then lied about their whereabouts. Her disloyalty was rewarded by sparing not only her, but her entire family when the city was conquered and its population exterminated by the armies of Israel.

Boaz's and Ruth's son, Obed, was only a quarter ethnic Jew. Of Obed's four grandparents, only Salmon was a blood descendant of Abraham. It is interesting to note that King David's grandfather would not have been "Jewish" enough to be granted citizenship by the nation of Israel prior to 1970. It was only then that immigration laws were amended to grant the grandchildren of Jews the right to citizenship. Even the Nazi regime that persecuted the Jews prior to and during World War II would not have classified Obed as a Jew. He would have been considered a *mischling* (which is German for cross-breed) by the Nuremburg Laws that the Nazis used to classify German citizens according to race. Individuals with partially Jewish heritage suffered discrimination under these immoral laws but were not subjected to the mass deportation and extermination that was the fate of those with purer Jewish pedigrees.

According to Jewish tradition, only people with Jewish mothers were considered Jews because bloodlines in traditional Judaism are traced through the mother's side of the family. Neither of Obed's grandmothers were ethnic Jews, thus making his Jewish ethnicity sketchy at best.

The Apostle Paul came to understand that even his impeccable Jewish pedigree was irrelevant to his status before God—that faith and faith alone was and still is the only criterion for citizenship. He was able to write with personal experience about his ancestry:

> *If anyone else has a mind to put confidence in the flesh, I far more: circumcised the eighth day, of the nation of Israel, of the tribe of Benjamin, a Hebrew of Hebrews; as to the Law, a Pharisee; as to zeal, a persecutor of the church; as to the righteousness which is in the Law, found blameless. But whatever things were gain to me, those things I have counted as loss for the sake of Christ* (Phil. 3:4-7).

Celebrate your heritage, enjoy your culture and family histories and give thanks to God for your ancestors. It is good to retell the stories of our grandparents, search the web for the family tree and get the oldest members of our family to write the names of people on the back of old photographs. It is important to know where we have come from. But we must temper our ethnic or religious pride by being mindful of the fact that God shows no preference to us because of our ethnicity or family's religious association. Even if we are third or fourth generation members of a church, or our dads are pastors or missionaries, we may be fluent in the language and know all the customs, but none of these things grants us citizenship in His Kingdom.

YOUR FATHER

The final reality all believers will live in is the reality of heaven, a timeless and tearless existence in perfect union with Christ and the Father. But unlike the world which is divided by language, custom and ethnicity, heaven will be a union of all the peoples of the world who have been redeemed by the Redeemer. Revelation describes the diversity of heaven this way:

> *"For Thou wast slain, and didst purchase for God with Thy blood men from every tribe and tongue and people and nation"* (Rev. 5:9).

I looked, and behold, a great multitude, which no one could count, from every nation and all tribes and peoples and tongues, standing before the throne and before the Lamb . . . (Rev. 7:9).

Until the day the above takes place, it is our privilege and duty to duplicate here on earth what we see in heaven.

Boaz is a prophetic picture of spiritual leaders who take the initiative to integrate outsiders into the existing community. It was at mealtime that Boaz says to Ruth, *"Come here"* (Ruth 2:14). His workers were not interested in getting to know the foreigner who was not part of their lunch circle, but Boaz cared about her. It is easy to imagine the surprised looks on the faces of the other workers as the alien is asked to have lunch with the owner, and we have already seen the prophetic significance of his personal invitation to share a meal together.

Also, there is this prophetic image of spiritual fathers and mothers validating the worth of individuals who are not part of the dominant culture. Leaders have an opportunity to model the heart of God by seeking to associate and fellowship with the Ruth-like humanity who sits alone in our communities and churches.

These prophetic images are the blueprint for the construction of our Christian communities. It is the Father's will for the Church to reflect here on earth the non-segregated reality of heaven, a reality that was foreshadowed throughout the Old Testament types, established as doctrine in the New Testament and revealed in the Book of Revelation as the ultimate reality of eternity.

The division of humanity that God orchestrated during the construction of the Tower of Babel has been replaced by the union of humanity in Christ. The Redeemer is drawing His Bride from every corner of the globe, and we have the opportunity and privilege of facilitating this multiethnic expression of our faith, not to mention the opportunity to eat some really interesting food at church suppers!

Our ability to embrace others is a "bell weather" behavior that is an accurate demarcation between Christian faith and Christian religion. No matter how mature a believer we think we are, or how mature others say we are, we are not mature in Christ if we hold elitist views of race and culture.

We dishonor our Father when we adopt church growth strategies that are the equivalent of the "separate but equal" policies used to justify the segregation of people in America not too long ago. We affirm equality before God theologically but maintain and guard our local assemblies from any encroachment by foreign cultures. The Church becomes a repository for language and culture rather than a visible expression of the Father's love for all peoples. Multiethnic church is not a cool, hip or sexy new model for church growth; it is an expression of Dad's desire to have all His kids around the same table at suppertime. It's a big table in a big house with a big backyard. Did I mention our Father's house is big?

Of course, mono-ethnic churches and communities are easier to maintain, and statistically they even tend to grow more rapidly than multiethnic expressions of faith. By nature, humans are xenophobic. That is, we are afraid of outsiders. We have this tactile fear of people groups we're not familiar with. In the natural, this fear has served humanity well; it allowed all of our ancestors to survive in times of war and invasion. Englishmen, for example, learned to run when they saw blond-haired guys in boats pulling into their harbors. Russians learned to run when they saw men with flat faces and slanted eyes ride into town on small horses. Spiritually, this fear is damaging to the Church because it causes us to run from meaningful relationships with people who are different than we.

Because multiethnic congregations are difficult to initiate and maintain, the responsibility for welcoming immigrants and assimilating them into the Kingdom lies with the mature residents of the Kingdom. I'm only an elder statesman when I behave like one.

The Apostle Paul wrote, *"For children are not responsible to save up for their parents, but parents for their children. And I will most gladly spend and be expended for your souls"* (2 Cor. 12:14). This is why I give up my seat to newcomers and try to sit with them at social events. It's why we let teenagers serve as worship leaders and attempt to play a wide variety of worship music styles. I am only a good citizen to the degree that I invest my energies in the training and installation of newcomers into authentic positions of responsibility within the Kingdom and the local body. Fear of immigration is one of the primary reasons there are so many mono-ethnic and mono-generational local churches.

When we view our communities and churches as our personal territory and our nation, it is natural for us to want to defend them from the invasion of people who listen to music we don't like and who place values on things in an order different than we do. Church signage nearly always includes the phrase, "Everyone welcome." But if churches were going to be really honest, they should probably say something like, "Everyone who is pretty much like us, who will embrace our distinctives, and conform to our practices is welcome."

We greet folks with the right words, but the condescending smiles on our tanned faces betray true feelings. They get back in their cars and sail away while we thumb through the latest "how to" book on church growth. Here is something I would like you to try as an experiment. Instead of inviting someone to church, invite them to your place for coffee or a meal. Be like Boaz who invited Ruth to have something to eat with him, welcoming her into his world. Opening our homes is often the first step in having our friends move into the Father's house.

CHAPTER 12
IRAs & 401(k)s

"My daughter, shall I not seek security for you,
that it may be well with you?" (RUTH 3:1).

Television ads for investment firms and insurance companies are scary. Disasters jump out of closets, poor planning slithers under our sheets, and retirement is coming up the basement steps to get us in the darkness of night. Naturally, these ads are aired during football games and golf tournaments. (The demographic consultants know full well that on Sunday afternoon the target audience is sprawled across couches from coast to coast.) Images of youthful retirees surfing with their grandsons at the beach house pixel on the plasma along with graduation ceremonies at universities with stone walls and lavish wedding receptions. Sometimes, these images make it hard for me to fall asleep at night, and when I finally do, they give me bad dreams.

These economic horror flicks are well-produced. Their graphic and explicit content will evoke responses from napping and nearly catatonic sports fans. Their message is simple and clear: Good people fully fund both of their kids' college savings accounts; good people have lots of money; good people work hard and invest wisely; bad people don't have second homes, and their kids work at the mall while going to state schools.

All of these ads invite us to come to their economic altar and be saved from financial disaster. So on Monday morning, we pick up the phone and run down the aisle to speak to the financial counselor waiting to hear our confession and receive our offering.

Perhaps that's why this prophetic picture of Ruth, the poor foreign-born gleaner becoming the financially secure wife of the redeemer, is so relevant to us today. The ageless urge to accumulate wealth combined with the fear of economic disaster has permeated not only our secular world but the Body of Christ.

Jesus understood the inherent power of money, and it is why He taught about it more than any other subject. Placing our resources at His disposal is a major component of coming to His altar and submitting to His authority in our lives. Our Redeemer enjoys fully funding the projects He has asked His Bride to participate in, and He relishes showering her with an abundance of provision. It's not His intention to keep His Bride barefoot and pregnant . . . well, pregnant, yes, but not barefoot! We enjoy His lavish provision but too often find ourselves fretting over our financial situations.

When I think about it (which I try not to do too often), my family is exposed to any number of uninsured risks that prowl about growling at our modest lifestyle. During fits of unbelief, I wonder if 20 years from now I will be one of those senior citizen greeters who paste stickers on children and slide shopping carts into the hands of the shoppers who waddle into the Wal-Mart. *Will I be one of those old people who didn't plan, didn't save and didn't go to the right school?* I wonder. There are darker moments when I think, *Will I be one of those poor saps who failed to scurry up the economic tree fast enough to escape the shame of being devoured by the economic lions I hear growling in the night?*

These concerns are not unique to middleclass Americans like me. People from every age and every part of the world are concerned about providing for their families and protecting their resources. Real live lions, for example, are an ever-present threat to the cattle that serve as the currency of the beautiful Massai people of East Africa—a people who measure wealth by the number of animals in the family herd. To protect their cattle from lions, families construct fences called *bomas* which are made by tightly weaving thorn bushes together, making it nearly impossible for hungry lions to attack their herds.

In the west, we weave our *bomas* with insurance policies and hedge funds that righteously protect our resources; protecting our resources is of course the right thing to do. It would be immoral for me not to pay the life insurance premium and risk impoverishing my wife and family in the event of my untimely death. It's proper for us to lock our doors at night, put our cattle inside our *bomas* and take the keys out of the car when we run into the store to grab a gallon of milk. Yet ultimately, there is a security that transcends our *bomas* and insurance policies. It is the best kind of security; it's the security of relationship.

RELATIONSHIP AND FEAR

For believers who are facing difficult financial times, the book of Ruth paints a comforting prophetic picture of a people whose relationship with their Redeemer quiets their fears of an uncertain future. In the pages of Scripture, we discover a prophetic image of a straight-backed Bride who walks through the global marketplace in complete security. She represents those who have entered the dynamic faith-based economy of His Kingdom, a land where trust is the currency. She foretells of a generation of savvy saints who have not been cowed into submission by the Godless doctrine of the financial purgatory being preached at economic revivals by the devotees of the almighty dollar. She bespeaks a Church who knows how to ignore the barkers who peddle the myth of economic security on the midway of national TV and is too wise to play the enemy's Three-card Monte.

Naomi wanted this kind of security for Ruth. Her motherly wisdom had not been completely extinguished by the ravages of bitterness and depression. Sometime between barley harvest and wheat harvest, she connected the dots and realized that Boaz was interested in more than just feeding his kinfolk. Sure, having the family farm redeemed would have given them temporary relief from their poverty, but matchmaking Ruth with the redeemer, now *that* would be real security for they wouldn't be hungry anymore. They wouldn't have to worry about where they would live and how they would pay their bills. They would no longer live in fear of economic disaster.

Seems like we hear the words "don't be afraid" our whole lives and come to believe that fear is bad. But actually fear is a good thing when we are afraid of the right things. Fear makes us hold onto the handrails when we go down steep steps and stay back from the edge of a cliff. It makes us squeeze our child's hand when we cross the road. It's why we involuntarily recoil at the sight of a snake we almost step on in the garden. We instinctively jump back (and sometimes scream) so we have time to correctly identify it as being a harmless garter snake or a deadly pit viper. God has endowed humankind by hard-wiring into our psyches an intuitive fear of things that might harm or kill us. These legitimate fears keep us alive.

Yet fearing the wrong things is debilitating, and misplaced fear shrinks the size of our universe. As we discussed previously in the chapter on Orpah, phobias of all kind have become a modern-day plague afflicting every strata of society. Anxiety and panic attacks are bombarding the souls of humanity. Non-specific, illegitimate, generic fear is crippling and limits our willingness to take risks in our pursuit of the Lord and the expansion of His Kingdom. Psychotropic medications are only marginally effective in addressing the symptoms of these fears and phobias and are certainly not a long-term strategy for successful living. These illegitimate fears are robbing us of the life He has destined us to live.

Our enemy has made us afraid of the wrong things. He is a bit like the clever English parents who used the fear of the Boogie Man to keep their kids quiet at night and sang this nasty lullaby to them before bed:

Baby, baby, naughty baby,
Hush! you squalling thing, I say;
Peace this instant! Peace! or maybe
Bonaparte will pass this way.
Baby, baby, he's a giant,
Black and tall as Rouen's steeple,
Sups and dines and lives reliant
Every day on naughty people.
Baby, baby, if he hears you
As he gallops past the house,
Limb from limb at once he'll tear you
Just as pussy tears a mouse.
And he'll beat you, beat you, beat you,
And he'll beat you all to pap:
And he'll eat you, eat you, eat you,
Gobble you, gobble you, snap! snap! snap![4]

During Napoleon's conquests of Europe, the British feared "Boney" or "Bogey" (as they called him) would cross the English Channel and invade their peaceful island. This fear of invasion was exploited by parents to make their children mind at bedtime. It is similar to how our deviously creative enemy has provoked us to feel terrified about things that exist only in our overstressed imaginations. Napoleon was only five feet six inches tall; he was not the giant cannibal portrayed in this verse. But we can only imagine the fear of toddlers who were scared into silence with this dark nursery rhyme.

Most of us are too old for nursery rhymes, so our enemy has enlisted an army of demonic propagandists who use their sharp tongues to goad our fears and exaggerate the stature of our economic Napoleons. He employs mercenary publicists who con us out of our birthright to rest peacefully in God's strong arms. They try to scare us so we don't cry out for His mercy in the night and don't raise our voices in hearty worship before dawn. We keep our faith shrouded in the bedcovers of convention and decorum, and hope our savings accounts will protect us. We don't embrace the Redeemer with our whole beings because we have been sung to sleep with scary lullabies, lullabies whose lyrics tell us that uninhibited and unreserved union with the Lord will lead us into poverty and financial ruin.

RELATIONSHIP AND CONTENTMENT

Naomi and Ruth were truly poor. They were poor by the Biblical definition of poor, not the make-believe poor dreamed up by the ad agencies that produce those horror ads for Smith Barney and Price Waterhouse. They went to bed hungry, and they woke up hungrier. They probably got wet if it rained, and we can be quite certain they weren't melting a quarter stick of butter and a half cup of brown sugar into their barley meal.

There was no food bank or emergency services for families in crisis. They were gleaners, bouncing about in the only flimsy safety net the culture afforded. It was ancient Israel's God-given welfare system that provided, at best, a very precarious existence. Crops ripen quickly, and there was competition for the scraps that were left behind. Compounding the equation was the reality that there were successive months when no crop was available at all. Gleaning was not meant to be a long-term strategy for living.

Even gleaning augmented by the special favors bequeathed upon Ruth by Boaz was not going to insure they made ends meet. Like anyone living close to the edge, they would have been the last to benefit from an economic boon or a bumper crop, and then the first to experience hardship when the harvest was not as plentiful or good times had ended. Living hand-to-mouth is living without margin, with no room for even a minor mishap or misstep.

Maybe you have experienced this kind of economic hardship. Maybe even now, you and your family feel like you're in an overloaded canoe, the water lapping the gunwales. With the frail vessel threatening to capsize at any moment, we shout, "Nobody move," and sit still. *Why did we throw out the mayonnaise jar?* you begin to wonder. *I could have scraped more out of it,* you worry. You batten down the hatches and count the change so you can buy gas.

This prophetic picture for the Body of Christ is not only one of provision based on relationship, but also one where expectations are tempered by Biblical standards. The standard for contentment is groceries and shelter: *"For we have brought nothing into the world, so we cannot take anything out of it either. And if we have food and covering, with these we shall be content"* (1 Tim. 6:7-8). We feel jilted or defrauded by the Lord only because our expectations of how He will provide for us are filtered through our distorted understanding of provision and wealth.

Ruth and Naomi were grateful and satisfied by an ephah of barley (equivalent to about a five gallon pail); in all likelihood, we would turn up our noses at such a provision and even question if we were being blessed, wondering if God still loved us. Be assured, He will provide for us and usually beyond what we have hoped. Yet our attitude must be one of gratefulness for having our most basic needs met, rather than the attitude of a spoiled child who is never content no matter how often his parents indulge his whims.

In an age where, at least here in America, praying not to eat too much has all but replaced thankfulness for daily bread, we would do well to reacquaint ourselves with His loving promise of basic provision for those who place His interests before their own. As Jesus said, *"'But seek first His Kingdom, and all these things shall be added to you. Do not be afraid, little flock, for your Father has chosen gladly to give you the Kingdom'"* (Luke 12:31-32).

This promise of provision must be moderated by spirits of contentment and thankfulness. Gratitude will empower us to exercise our faith in a concerted effort to expand the Kingdom, rather than exercising it to acquire the latest designer clothes to adorn our ever-expanding waistlines. Contentment will give us the desire to own cars that don't cost more than building an entire medical clinic in the third world. Contentment will insure we are not plastering over the old-fashioned lathe of greed with the stucco of religious jargon.

RELATIONSHIP AND RETIREMENT

All too often my financial burdens are actually just the illegitimate weight of cultural expectations that have subtly attached themselves to my soul. Saving vast sums of money for a carefree retirement is another such illegitimate expectation. His promise to provide does extend even into old age when our physical strength declines and our mental prowess wanes, *"Even to your old age, I will be the same, and even to your graying years I shall bear you!"* (Is. 46:4).

The promise of provision into our golden years is part of every believer's faith portfolio. We don't want to be a burden to our children, but this obsession with not outliving our money is weighing down our souls and siphoning off some of our most talented and gifted workers who feel compelled by these false expectations to pursue more lucrative secular careers.

Today, I want to wrap my arms around Him and enjoy His provision. The promise of daily bread, the promise to supply all my needs and even the promise to provide for me in my old age need to be woven into the fabric of my being—woven into my psyche like the golden threads which were woven into the garments of the priests (Ex. 39:3).

When the fear of economic disaster keeps me up at night, these are truths I need to know in the deepest recesses of my soul. I need this assurance when my dreams are turned into nightmares by the whale and bull mascots of the insurance and investment companies who spin their scary stories of shame and guilt around the flat-screen campfire in my living room just before bedtime. The truth is not what they are telling me. God is going to provide for my family now and in the future the way He always has, and we will be fine. I'm also thinking I need to stop watching those little horror movies on Sunday afternoon; they really do make me afraid.

CHAPTER 13
That's Not Barley

"'Wash yourself therefore, and anoint yourself and put on your best clothes . . . .'
So she went down to the threshing floor and did according to all that her
mother-in-law had commanded her. When Boaz had eaten and drunk
and his heart was merry, he went to lie down at the end of the heap of grain;
and she came secretly, and uncovered his feet and lay down. And it happened
in the middle of the night that the man was startled and bent forward;
and behold, a woman was lying at his feet" (RUTH 3:3, 6-8).

Vulnerability is the essence of spirituality. Choosing to place ourselves in situations that involve real risk is a prerequisite for reproductive faith. Vulnerability is sleeping with the doors of our souls unlocked. Vulnerability is driving without the safety belt of secrecy. Vulnerability is keeping the angels on the sidelines while the guards pull out your beard. Vulnerability is letting people see the sweat mix with the blood. Vulnerability is crawling under the blanket with a man in the middle of the night. It's a risky business. Sometimes, we get married; sometimes, we get crucified. But every time we make ourselves vulnerable, we awaken the passions of the Redeemer.

Ruth took a colossal risk; she gambled on the character of Boaz. If Boaz was not the real deal, if he was some sort of religious showman, she was in trouble. Boaz could have indulged in a one-night romp in the grain. After all, Ruth had come to him and asked him to spread his cover over her. I mean, what did she expect? Any guy would do the same thing. She was the one who sneaked to the barn in the middle of the night, and she knew he had been drinking. The last thing she would have seen was the Star of David bumper sticker on his chariot as it pulled out of the driveway in the morning.

Ruth also risked being strung along by Boaz. He could have manipulated her into becoming his long-term mistress with vague promises of marriage or redemption somewhere off in the future. In the meantime, as long as she made regular midnight visits to the farm, Naomi and she would be able to pay the mortgage. She might even find some expensive gifts at her door occasionally, special tokens of appreciation. Of course, the timing of their union would never be quite right, difficulties and situations ever postponing and delaying the wedding that would never happen. She could have become a kept woman, safely tucked away in his deep pockets. Economic prosperity in exchange for infidelity is the age-old song and dance routine.

Thankfully, Boaz was a man of integrity. Ruth believed that Boaz was safe, and her conviction proved to be correct. She was completely vulnerable, and he didn't take advantage of her in either of these illicit ways. His character had been progressively and accurately revealed to her over the preceding months. He was the real deal; he was the same man at midnight as he was at noon. Integrity is expensive; we have to pay to get it and pay to keep it. Boaz was a man who valued his integrity more than his urge to capitalize on the sexual opportunity lying at his feet. This time his integrity cost him some quick satisfaction.

REAL MEN

As a resister to temptation, Boaz is the perfect type of Christ. Neither of them was nor is a fornicator. Like Boaz, our Redeemer legitimizes our intimacy with Him by allowing us to enter into covenant with Him first. Intimate relations with Him are not possible until we are wed to Him in the bonds of Holy Covenant. "In sickness and in health, for richer for poorer, for better or worse, till death do us part." He said His vows 2,000 years ago on the altar that was shaped like a cross. He waits for us to say our "I do's" before He will carry us across the threshold of His Kingdom. Sex before marriage is not part of His plan; we don't share His bed until we have been united to Him in holy matrimony.

Maybe you're uncomfortable with the image of a Redeemer who is really tempted. Maybe the thought of Boaz, who is an Old Testament picture of Christ being sexually tempted, is offensive to you. Maybe you have mistakenly believed or been taught that the temptations of Christ in the wilderness were not real temptations. Maybe you understand His experience in the wilderness to have been more like a quiz that He already knew the answers to rather than a series of real exams. Maybe you see Him breezing through the wilderness like cars with the easy pass gliding through the toll booths. Slow up a little, stay in lane and off we go again, a barely noticeable interruption in our commute. But this was not the case; both Boaz and Jesus were really tempted.

The Scriptures are explicit concerning the reality of the temptations Jesus faced. He understands experientially, not just theologically or intellectually, the trauma of temptation. He understands temptation because He became a real man.

> *Therefore, He had to be made like His brethren in all things, that He might become a merciful and faithful high priest in things pertaining to God, to make propitiation for the sins of the people. For since He Himself was tempted in that which He has suffered, He is able to come to the aid of those who are tempted* (Heb. 2:17-18).

> *For we do not have a high priest who cannot sympathize with our weaknesses, but one who has been tempted in all things as we are, yet without sin. Let us therefore draw near with confidence to the throne of grace, that we may receive mercy and find grace to help in time of need* (Heb. 4:15-16).

The Bible tells us that Jesus was tempted because it is essential for us to know this. We need to know that He is not a spiritual android—something that looks like flesh and blood but is not. How tragic it would be if when we got under His blanket we discovered He had no pulse, no heart beat and that his skin was just some sort of spongy synthetic imitation. Thankfully, we get to hear His heart beat; we get to touch Him. His blood was warm when poured out of Him. The Word became flesh to emancipate our flesh from the bondage and obligation to obey its lusts. He knows the power of our addictions and our unwholesome inclinations because He was tempted with every temptation ever experienced by all of humanity. He sympathizes with our weakness because He has walked our path in real skin.

The Scriptures don't tell us that Boaz was tempted by the presence of an attractive, smooth-skinned, sweet smelling young woman lying at his feet in the middle of the night. It is possible that, after Boaz asked her to spend the night at his feet and told her he would look into the redemption thing in the morning, he just fluffed his grain, rolled over and went back to sleep. It's possible, and if you want to believe that is how things went that night, that's fine. However, the text describes a much more volatile and sexually-charged situation. Evidence of his romantic interest in Ruth is revealed by the fact that he becomes her redeemer and marries her the very next day. Make no mistake about it; he wanted to sleep with Ruth.

Boaz and Ruth are great role models for engaged couples in every age and every place. They had all the opportunity any couple could have wanted—a little wine, a blanket and a comfortable private place in which to enjoy each other's company. Boaz's and Ruth's abstinence until marriage is an excellent example of sexual purity for any couple. Two things, of course, stand out in this account. First, that it is possible to abstain from sexual sin even in situations when the temptation is great and no one else would know about it. Second, the engagement was really short. For serious-minded Christians who value their purity, these are good lessons.

ALL DRESSED UP AND ONE PLACE TO GO

Getting dressed up for a special occasion is an important event for a girl; I know this because I'm a husband, and I'm a father of three girls. My experience has taught me to keep a safe distance from the process, and I learned the hard way not to make any suggestions. If you're new to the husband or father of daughters business, let me save you some grief. Comments like, "You look fine to me. Don't worry about it," or "I don't see what the big deal is" and "Hurry up we're going to be late" are best left unsaid, unless you like the sound of slamming doors. But even from a respectful distance, I have been able to observe all the effort, all the stress, all the inevitable mixing, matching, tweezing and crimping that takes place in the hours before a gal is ready to make her public appearance.

Any female visitor at Naomi and Ruth's place on the evening Ruth was getting ready for her tryst with Boaz would have immediately grasped what was going on. Without explanation, they would have instantly known that Ruth was going somewhere important. They would have heard Ruth asking Naomi's opinion on clothing options; gals have an intuitive understanding that such decisions are best made together.

The women in my life have strong opinions when it comes to what looks best on each other and speak an unknown tongue of fashion. Somehow, they know if someone is a spring or fall, summer or winter. Furthermore, they understand what accessories go with what outfits. They know when hair should be up or down, straight or curled. How they know all this is a mystery to me; all I know is that it's not easy being a girl.

But what would have been most perplexing to a visitor that evening was Ruth was not going to be seen in public. It would have been difficult for anyone to grasp that she wasn't getting dressed to be seen by more than one person. If we were privy to such a scene today, we would be thinking a prom or party or anniversary date at a favorite restaurant was in the offing. But Ruth wasn't getting dressed up for a reception or awards ceremony; she was getting dressed up to risk everything in a gambit to kindle the passions of the one man who could make everything right. She got cleaned up, dressed up and oiled up, to garner the favor and win the affections of her redeemer.

If masculine attention was all that Ruth was after, she most certainly picked the wrong time of day and the wrong place for that. If she was fishing for just any husband, she could have trolled the open waters of Bethlehem's singles scene. She could have placed herself in situations where eligible suitors could get a good look at her—public places where she could mingle with members of the opposite sex, where she could have flirted and enjoyed the flattery of men who could appreciate her efforts to look her very best. Of course, she was focused on only one man; his attention was her only concern.

In this respect, Ruth is the perfect picture of the Bride of Christ aspiring to be a people whose only care is about looking their best for their Redeemer, a people who are unconcerned about what other men think about their appearance; a people who ignore the whistles and cat calls of this age as we walk toward the threshing floor. Yes, we're supposed to be a confident, soon-to-be

Bride, whose insecurities don't compel us to seek the attention or approval of this present age. We're supposed to be a one-man woman who no longer cares about or even notices the gauntlet of attractive and eligible suitors who line her path.

Before we tag along with Ruth on her encounter with Boaz, I would like to offer one other observation. It's very likely Ruth was still wearing the same clothes she put on that night when she got married the next day. From a purely logistical standpoint, it didn't make sense for her to go through the whole primping process again, especially in light of the fact that Naomi was telling her, *"Wait, my daughter, until you know how the matter turns out, for the man will not rest until he has settled it today"* (Ruth 3:18). I'm not sure, but it's possible that Ruth was starting to take off her good clothes that morning and Naomi told her to wait, to sit tight for a while because that day was going to be her wedding day. It's an intriguing image of the Bride of Christ waiting for her Redeemer wearing her best clothes.

THE MIDDLE OF THE NIGHT

Boaz was a hardworking farmer, working late one night to process his crops for market. Like most self-employed people, he stayed on the job as long as necessary and picked up the slack when employees weren't available or called in sick. He was successful because he personally worked hard and watched over his investment. As a single man, he probably spent more than one night on the threshing floor when it was too late or he was too tired to go home. So like many other nights, he had supper, drank a bit of wine, snuffed out the lamp and fell asleep.

Meanwhile, young Ruth was watching him through a crack in the wall or beyond the circle of light around the threshing floor. Threshing floors were located in breezy places so farmers could separate the valuable grain from the worthless chaff by tossing both up into the moving air. The grain would be piled in the open or under a rustic shed to protect it from rain or dew. This is the place Ruth snuck up to, the place where she watched him finish up his chores and eat a simple dinner; and before he killed the lights, she watched him lie down.

Then she waited. Bethlehem nodded off, windows went black in random spurts, latches were checked, and dogs circled their resting places. Another night fell. Out in the field, alone in the dark, she began to lose her nerve, thought about going back home and calling the whole thing off. Her mind thumbed through all the possible scenarios, all the possible outcomes that the night would reveal. She kept waiting.

She wouldn't have known the scientific differences between REM sleep and Alpha sleep, but she knew enough to wait long enough to be sure that he was completely out before she crept near him. Maybe she was still wondering why she had on her good clothes while waiting alone in the dark. The breeze grew cooler; the sounds of crickets and the redeemer's slow regular breaths filled the air. It was time to take a risk.

She began inching toward the threshing floor and suddenly stopped; a dog barked in the distance. She heard Boaz's breathe sputter, his lips smacked, and he mumbled something incoherent. Her heart stopped. She heard him roll over, and every muscle in her body attempted to strangle her bones.

After a few moments, his breathing resumed the cadence of deep sleep. She let out her breath silently and slowly. She resumed her slow-motion stalk, each little foot slowing bore her shifting weight. Time itself crawled to a stop; she did not know how long it had taken to traverse the distance to his feet. *Was it an hour, or was it a lifetime?* Gently, his blanket was pealed back. She lay down and stared into the black, stars burned in silent ovation while she awaited her destiny.

Meanwhile, Boaz was innocently enjoying the dreamless regeneration of the first hours of sleep. His consciousness transferred command of his body to the involuntary control center hours ago. All five senses had gone below deck to allow his mind to be debugged and defragged without interruption. Any information coming through the senses was rerouted into the dream machine, the place where his mind could process the data without awaking him. The night crew had settled into its shift, quietly guarding the precious hours of rest. But as the night passed, his sleep grew more shallow; consciousness swam closer to the surface of slumber's sea. Strange and novel information was starting to leak past the security team on the bridge.

For some time, the feet of the sleeping redeemer had been futilely attempting to get a message through to the comatose conscience. At first they reported a simple temperature variation, but then they tried to tell him they had made first contact with a life form they had never encountered before. His subconscious ignored the initial reports; no point in waking up the big guy about some nonsense reported by a chilly toe on the front lines. But the reports kept coming in. The night watch was starting to get jittery; there was something down there; something was definitely wrong. In a final attempt to stay asleep, his mind instructed his feet to gather more data by probing the unknown object.

The feet moved in; calloused soles and clumsy toes were unaccustomed to this kind of work. Hands were usually sent on this kind of sensitive mission. Predictably, they transmitted confusing intelligence data back to the mental command center. Reports about an alien body lying off the stern confused the awaking mind. Toes poked the warm, soft, actually, very soft mystery. They didn't know what it was, but one thing was sure—it wasn't barley they were feeling. *Wait a minute, captain,* the nose next reported a sweet smell in the air. *Battle stations, sound the alarm! We have confirmed a bogey at six o'clock!* His eyes snapped open; he twisted forward in the night.

He called out, "Who are you?"

"I'm Ruth . . . I'm Susan . . . I'm Tom . . . I'm David . . . I'm Bob . . . I'm James . . . I'm Mindy . . . I'm Sam . . . I'm Mike . . . I'm José . . . I'm Serge . . . I'm Juan . . . I'm Marie . . . I'm Alex . . . I'm Bill . . . I'm Jamie . . . I'm Peter . . . I'm Saul . . . I'm Terry . . . I'm Jenifer. I'm everyone and everybody who has ever needed to know that there was a Redeemer. I'm every lost soul who doesn't have a home and has nowhere to go. I'm humanity, and I'm asking that You spread Your cover over my cold body. I'm everyone who has ever stared into the darkness and wondered if God would wake up and take care of them."

CHAPTER 14
The Merry Redeemer

*"When Boaz had eaten and drunk and his heart was merry,
he went to lie down at the end of the heap of grain . . ."* (RUTH 3:7).

Boaz was happy. After a long day of work, he was able to wash down a
late night meal with a few swigs of wine and go to sleep with a merry
heart. We can see him kicking off his sandals and unrolling his blanket.
He scoops out a cozy mattress in the soft grain, lays back, jiggles his hips and
shakes his shoulders. The grain shifts to receive his form. His mouth opens,
his eyes shut, and he draws in a double dose of night air that gets stuck under
his chin before it is expelled in a day-ending yawn. He massages his face, his
lips smack and then curl into a smile. This ancient image flickers in our
minds' eyes. The Scriptures give us a glimpse of a man with a merry heart—
a Biblical picture of who he is.

But there is a problem. The idea that this type of Christ was merry has
me shaking my head; the thought of a merry Redeemer makes me feel nervous. What if just maybe I have stepped into an arena of theological presump-
tion that no longer correctly recognizes His Holiness?

I ask myself these questions: *Is God happy? If so, how often is He happy? If
He is happy, then why am I often sad? How can we be joyful and smile while so
much evil permeates our world? If the Gospel means good news, then why do so
many Christians wear faces that make them look like their dog just died?* Perhaps
these were the thoughts I had as a child but was simply too young to put them
into words.

THE PICTURE DOESN'T LIE

A few years ago my mom sent me a collection of my old grade school photographs. You know the kind where 23 kids are arranged in three rows. Tall boys

and one awkward girl stand in the back of the picture. The short kids in front are sitting with crisscrossed legs on the floor, and a student seated in the middle of the picture holds a placard with the grade and teacher's name written in movable plastic type. Off to the side, a neatly dressed woman politely smiles into a camera from behind glasses that probably seemed like a good idea at the time. I was surprised that I could recall the names of most of the kids after so many years.

The photos were like electrical probes poking into different parts of my brain—the kind of probes seen in the brains of others on TV science shows. There the surgeons are able to evoke involuntary responses by stimulating specific parts of the cerebral cortex. They animate their patients like marionettes by pulling the electrical strings of their exposed gray matter.

Those photos pulled out my personal files that were opened for the first time in many years, and I involuntarily pointed and called out the names of old classmates to my wife and kids who were fascinated by these pictures. The toothless smiles of second graders transported me to the once-upon-a-time land of kick ball and note passing.

I don't think I would have ever noticed the one thing that was constant in each of the pictures. From the early black-and-white photos of first and second grade to the color photos that were the high-tech replacement by the sixth grade, there was one thing that remained the same. It was painfully obvious, but I never saw it until a close friend who was looking at the pictures a few days after we got them in the mail innocently stated the obvious.

In every picture, all the kids were smiling or grinning at the photographer, all the kids looked happy except one—me. From kindergarten to sixth grade, my sullen face stared into the camera. In some of the pictures, I even looked angry while in others I just looked pathetic—a sad little face in a class of well-tended children growing up in the abundant lap of suburbia. I don't know why I was such a sad kid; I have great parents, and I lived in a nice neighborhood in an affluent small town. I'm not sure anyone really ever noticed. Maybe someone tried to intervene; maybe I just didn't like pictures. I don't know.

What I do know is that after our friend said what my wife was too kind to say, I was transported back to the world my soul had conveniently forgotten. It's as if I was blinded by some sort of emotional cataract that made it impossible to see what was so clear to everyone else. The pictures evoked emotions I found embarrassing. Those pictures became a faded mirror rediscovered in the attic of my soul—a dusty image that allowed me to feel my way back into the shadows of my personal history and experience it anew. They helped me to feel some of the internal pain my childish face was not sophisticated enough to disguise.

I quickly shuffled through the pictures and realized my friend's observations were spot on. I saw myself for who I really was as a child; tears welled up into my eyes. I saw myself and understood how easy it was for the predators who later stalked my soul to recognize me as an easy victim. I looked at my childish face and instantly understood why not too many years later I would anesthetize myself with any substance that would numb the pain of my tortured soul—numb the pain of my personal inquisitor's medieval experiments which were designed to cripple my mind and turn me into catatonic fool of his Godless domain. I guess I just never understood at the time how much pain I was in, how excruciating existence was without the hope of redemption.

THE DARK PLAGUE

Unfortunately, my experience was not unique. Behind many of the smiling faces of my classmates hid the same feelings, the same thoughts and the same pain. Today, sadness and depression have reached epidemic levels. In September of 2007, the World Health Organization released a comprehensive study of depression that involved people from over 60 countries. News agencies across the globe reported what many already knew—namely that depression is more disabling than many physical conditions.[5]

The past 20 years have seen sales of both legal and illegal mood-altering drugs skyrocketing while a debilitating fog of depression has grown ever thicker and settled down upon most of humanity. A thick cloud of sadness has obscured our view of heaven and left us sullen and despondent.

Sadness and depression seem like a logical consequence for folks who are unredeemed. When I was trapped in a worldview that denied the existence of a knowable God—and I believed there was no real purpose for this life or reward in the next one—I was depressed. What perplexes me is that I found myself living under that same old cloud—even after I believed.

I've experienced unusually long and gloomy seasons that are not easily explained by the usual suspects of death, sickness, disobedience or spiritual burden that have temporarily weighed down my soul. I know my experience was not unique. Many of my believing friends find themselves under a perpetually overcast sky, living beneath an unbroken gray blanket of hopelessness and depression that is enveloping the earth.

I'm not sure where sadness ends and depression starts. I'm not qualified to draw the line between mental health and mental illness. Before we examine the revelation of a happy Redeemer, I would like to allay any of your fear or concerns I'm going to suggest that there is a simple remedy for everyone who suffers from depression or experiences discouragement or sadness. I'm not attempting to diagnose anyone's situation. I'm not going to suggest a prescriptive multistep self-help program that will fix us. If you or a loved one suffers from chronic depression, you're rightfully bristling at any suggestion that there is a simplistic religious fix to this complicated malady.

What I'm proposing and what I'm convinced of is that our image of our heavenly Father and Redeemer has been distorted and skewed. I believe that this distortion has contributed to the widespread acceptance of sadness and depression as being normal. I believe that the enemy has attempted to confiscate the pictures of the Redeemer wearing a smile and has allowed only the images of His anger or grief to be viewed by His people.

"MIRROR, MIRROR ON THE WALL . . ."

From my perspective, it is as if the enemy of our souls has bent the mirror through which we catch our glimpses of eternity. Somehow, our adversary has stolen our old ones and replaced them with concave mirrors that have flipped smiles into frowns. The enemy has hung not-so-much-fun funhouse mirrors in our minds and our houses of worship that have confused and disorientated us. Giant murals of an angry Sovereign tower over our religious cities; we are afraid to look up and scurry back to our gray flats and double-lock the door.

The thought of seeing eternity through a mirror is not the problem. It is a Biblical metaphor used by the Apostle Paul to help us understand the partial nature of revelation in this present age (1 Cor. 13:12). Ancient mirrors could only produce a fuzzy dull image because the technology of the day was fairly rudimentary. These mirrors were not able to reflect the sharp crisp images we see when we brush our teeth in the morning. Even though the image Paul wrote about is incomplete and fuzzy, it is not a twisted or distorted reflection of who God is.

We have a Redeemer who smiles. The Bible tells us of the Lord Jesus Christ who was anointed *"with the oil of gladness above [His] companions"* (Heb. 1:9). Like Boaz, He has a merry heart. The smile on the Savior's face is not like the painted smile of the sad-eyed clown. It's not like the professional smile of the receptionist at your dentist's office, and it's certainly not the toothy smile of the perpetually positive motivational speaker. To be honest, I'm not sure exactly what His smile looks like because I haven't actually seen Him smile yet. But I've felt Him smile, and my spirit has heard Him laugh.

But there is a problem. The Bible also says that our Redeemer is *"a man of sorrows, and acquainted with grief"* (Is. 53:3). If we're honest, I think many of us are simply more comfortable with this mental picture of God. We prefer to carry only these pictures of the Lord in our wallets and hang them in our living rooms because we feel guilty. And because we feel guilty, it only seems logical that our Father would appear peeved in the theater of our minds—ready to fly off the handle at the slightest provocation.

As a result, we tiptoe around the house hoping He doesn't notice us; we keep our eyes on the floor when He speaks. Our moments of levity come when we're sure we're out of His earshot and view. We smoke behind the garage and goof around with our friends, but when we come into His house, we take on a different posture and put on our church face. Party's over boys and girls, time to get serious and take what we have coming to us—time to pay up for our sins and receive the weekly tongue-lashing and guilt trip we so rightly deserve.

Yeah, this is how we perceive Him. He gave His life for us, and now we need to keep up our end of the deal. We sing songs about a debt we can't pay, but, by golly, we need to make an installment on the account every waking moment of our sorry existence. The collection agency bangs at our conscience's door continually asking for more—more money, more time, more witnessing, more prayer, more of everything. On Sunday morning, His enforcers pace angrily across the stage, castigating the lazy army with verbal drubbings—lamenting the loss of territory, warning us about the pending destruction of our nation. These are angry older brother types who seem to enjoy traumatizing younger siblings with weekly reminders that Dad will be home soon. We are terrified that we're just a few seconds away from getting what we have coming to us.

Sadly, this is how His representatives often portray Him. The picture they portray and we so readily accept is that of a not-so-merry Redeemer. We all seem to intuitively agree His heart is heavy and so He must also be pacing the halls of heaven grieving the loss of territory and pounding His fist on the map. He is furious with His incompetent generals; there is blood in His eyes, and His patience has just about run out. We nervously slide our tribute onto the altar, hoping that it's enough to stave off His wrath for another six days. Our faces are soon molded into this image; we begin to take on the very appearance of our angry Leader our minds have imagined.

The reason I know so much about all this is because I was one of those self-appointed goons who believed our Father was always angry. I enjoyed the thoughts of His righteous retribution and revenge. I looked into the pages of Scripture and saw only the angry God of the Old Testament and the rivers of blood of the book of Revelation. A large part of me was angry and frustrated, and most of me felt nervously guilty when I or anyone else was getting a bit too merry.

I was getting pretty good at wiping smiles off of faces. Then a series of events took some of the bend out of the mirror that I was looking at eternity through. One of these events happened over 12 years ago, and the benefits are still with me. So I have some confidence that it was not just a temporary fix to my brokenness. Besides, my wife says that I've been a lot easier to live with since then; so it must be true.

CLYDESDALE COLLISION

I was discouraged again. The same old pattern of cyclical discouragement and depression was repeating itself for the umpteenth time. It was like a mental flu that I kept getting re-infected with. You know how it is when you're catching a cold or flu, one minute you're feeling okay and then there is an ache in your lower back or twinge in your throat. A sneeze, a cough and the "oh no I'm getting sick" thought that we keep bottled up in denial. Eventually, we put a thermometer in our mouths to confirm what we already knew. We collapse into bed, call in sick and pray it passes quickly.

One of the things that usually helped me recuperate from these soul viruses was a camping trip. I would go up into the attic and get my backpack or come home one day to find it next to the back door. My wife always knew when it was time for me to spend a few days in solitary timeout. A tent in the woods became an operating room where I could lance my wounds and squeeze out the infected emotional puss.

Salty tears did a decent job of washing out the junk that was making me sick. It was a quick fix that vented the pressure but never cured the source. It was on one of these retreats that I had an unusual experience.

It was early spring, and there were still large patches of snow in the forest. I set up camp in an old sand pit that was on the edge of a wilderness area where I had been lost in previous excursions. The twisted topography of that area was the perfect geographic reflection of what was going on in my soul. Abandoned, cold, forlorn, it evoked a melancholy that brought my symptoms to a fever pitch, a geographic sweat lodge whose lancets would stab my swollen pustules.

To distract myself, I had gone fishing one afternoon in the tail of the hydroelectric dam that was not too far away. I fished till almost dark and caught nothing. I gave up, cast my last cast and started to trudge back to my campsite. I was despondent and blurted out in angry frustration, "God, I just want to drink a beer!" Yes, me, the puritanical preacher had surrendered; I had broken under the stress and asked to be anesthetized for the painful puss-letting that was soon to happen.

And then it appeared. Right there in the middle of the trail amid patches of crystallized snow was a 22-ounce unopened bottle of beer. I stood over it in disbelief. I thought, *NO WAY!* (Just like you're thinking now.) I stooped down and picked it up, held it up to see if it was full, tried the cap to see if it had been opened. I looked around the empty forest, looking for the clown who was playing this practical joke on me. The only thing there was an empty forest, a sad preacher and a full bottle.

I almost ran back to camp. Like a shoplifter trying to put distance between himself and the convenience store, I trotted down trail, over the wooden bridge, up the washed out dirt road and back to the sandpit to have dinner and a beer with Jesus.

I put the bottle in a small stream fed by melting snow, stoked the fire and heated up my MRE (Meal, Ready-to-Eat) that I was having for dinner. I could have counted on one hand the number of alcoholic beverages I had consumed in the previous 15 years, and so the effect of those first few swigs was pretty intense. It wasn't like I was nursing the beer I drank at my sister's wedding. The truth is I gulped down about half of those 22 ounces in one pull.

So there I sat, all alone, eating my mystery meat in the light of a roaring fire. The stars had come out, and the temperatures were falling. Time passed at its proper pace. I took a deep breath and felt happy; I wasn't frustrated or sad. An unfamiliar contentment filled me.

Then Jesus asked me a couple of questions. Just for the record, I did not hear an audible voice or see His form in smoke. But there came a couple of questions, succinctly-worded questions, the kind of questions only He can ask. If He has asked you a question, you know exactly the kind of verbal economy I'm talking about. First He asked me, "Jeff, do you know anyone who lives what you preach?"

I was tempted to lie but was under the influence of domestic screw-top truth serum. So I did the smart thing and answered an embarrassed and honest, "No."

In fact, neither me nor anyone else could actually live out the religious template I so sincerely but mistakenly believed would lead us into greater grace. I had created a model believer who passed muster on every level. And even though I acknowledged that theologically speaking we were incapable of attaining to this temporal perfection, I kept espousing this unachievable model in hopes of inspiring greater devotion and passion in both myself and those who listened to my teaching and preaching. My distorted image of God had imprinted itself in my ministry.

Then He asked me the second question, "Then why do you preach it?"

I have been trying to correctly answer this question with my life and ministry ever since. Trying to accurately convey the mystery of how being close to the Redeemer produces all the behaviors, thoughts and feelings we are unable to manufacture or produce ourselves—that there is a place of repose and repast where we experience a levity, a supernatural contentment that delivers us from evil. There were no more questions that night.

In the morning, there were still some embers in the fire that my breath was able to coax back to life. There was pretty heavy frost on the ground; the cowboy coffee I had boiled up on the fire warmed me to the bone. I wish I would have saved that brown bottle; we could have turned it into a modern spiritual relic.

But there are two things I still have from that night. One is a deep and abiding conviction that He is not as angry, mad or frustrated as I used to think He was. The second is the smile that is often on my face.

CHAPTER 15
Free Lunch

*"So she lay at his feet until morning and rose before one could recognize another;
and he said, 'Let it not be known that the woman came to the threshing floor.'
Again he said, 'Give me the cloak that is on you and hold it.'
So she held it, and he measured six measures of barley and laid it on her.
Then she went into the city"* (RUTH 3:14-15).

*"'I sent you to reap that for which you have not labored;
others have labored and you have entered into their labor'"* (JOHN 4:38).

Ruth is driving against traffic; she is headed home as Bethlehem is getting up to go to work. She is like the phantoms veiled behind the glare of oncoming headlights who zip down empty lanes on the other side of the median while we sit in traffic and sip coffee on our way to work.

While the city slumbered, she lay awake at his feet. Now in the dim predawn, she steals home with a harvest she didn't work for, an anonymous silhouette carefully toting a makeshift sack of barley.

Quickly and quietly her sandaled feet pad her home; a few more yards and no one will know where she's been. No one will know that the night before she discovered a place where the harvest was given away. No one will know, not yet.

She breaks into a trot as she comes up the path to the house. The door has been left ajar; she slips inside, closing it with her back. She leans against the door panting, perspiring from walking so quickly with her load. She is winded from the exhilaration of spending the night with a man and then sneaking home like a wayward wife.

She sets down her bundled haul and peeks out the window. All clear, no one has tailed her, the operation a success. The only evidence that she has not spent the night in her own bed is her dew-drenched clothes and pile of grain on the floor.

The sun moves over the horizon, the mist beating a hasty retreat from its presence. Small sandal prints in the damp grass are forever erased, the sun's heat wiping away all evidence of the risky tryst.

Ruth is a prophetic picture of a people who have discovered a different spiritual economy. She is a prophetic prototype of people who spend time in secret places and come home just before dawn with dew on their clothes and lunch on their backs. She discovers a place where the soul-breaking nature of religious labor is exchanged for the life-giving partnership of harvesting with the one who owns the field. She draws a prophetic picture of a people who discover the place where the harvest is given away.

I love this picture of Ruth getting lunch for free. I love Jesus' promise of reaping a harvest we did not labor for. But getting something for nothing just doesn't seem right. It cuts across my sensibilities and experience; I was trained to believe there is no such thing as a free lunch. There is always a shipping or handling fee, or an unexplained charge that pops up on next month's credit card statement. We know that work is a holy gift that is God-ordained and God-applauded. How is it possible then that Ruth escapes the bondage of menial labor and enters into an economy where lunch is really free? Where is this place of reaping without laboring that Jesus spoke about?

McMANNA

From my perspective, congregations sometimes look more like restaurants than spiritual entities—places that are feeding the Bread of Heaven the best way they know how. There is deep fried, stir fried and country fried manna. There is manna tartar for the bravest and grilled manna for those on a diet and manna flambé for those that like a little fire with their meal. There are even manna splits for dessert. I love manna splits; they coat the manna so deep in sugary goodness you don't even taste the manna.

Manna eateries come in all shapes and sizes, and fit every budget. From the franchised manna outlets near the mall or highway to the candlelit gourmet kind, where one needs a tie and reservations to get seated. I'm thankful for the variety of places where God's people can get a taste of heaven—places where they can find the Bread of Life. It's an imperfect analogy for modern churches, to be sure, but seems to capture some of the dynamics we experience.

This unbiblical image of the Body casts people in different roles. The pastor plays the part of restaurateur, head chef, manager or cook. (The pastor's role varies significantly depending on the size and style of the church he or she runs.) The deacons or ministry heads are the wait staff, scurrying about bussing tables, refilling water and asking if everything is okay. The worship team, of course, provides the music and ambiance. And let's not forget the congregation; they play the part of paying customer.

The competition is fierce in both the restaurant and the church businesses, establishments vying for customer loyalty and good reviews. Patrons are notoriously unstable in both these industries. One bad meal will often send them searching for another place to dine, another place to get their ration of Heaven's Bread. It's interesting that, in many communities today, there are as many churches as there are restaurants. Churches fill virtually every ecclesiastical, ethnic and theological niche imaginable. Religious consumers are able to sample the religious cuisine of hundreds of blends of theology and practice. As in the restaurant business, a church's success is often contingent upon many natural factors, including location, service and hours of operation.

But perhaps the most profound similarity between restaurants and religious organizations is the pivotal role played by the owner or leader in both these businesses. Like Ruth, we too live in an era of Judges, a time when the success of the ancient nation was contingent on the presence of a charismatic leader known as a judge. Similarly, the successes of our present-day spiritual enterprises seem directly correlated to the devotion, talent and energies of our own local Gideons and Sampsons. Leader-centric movements are generational; this is why, when the footprint of the judge erodes, the enemy moves back in to plunder the land. It's why ministries fade after dad dies.

Nonetheless, we need to be very thankful for all those the Lord has raised up to lead us—thankful that God has given us local judges who use their skill and talent to promote the Gospel of Christ. However, our corporate ambition should be to enter into that place where the Body more evenly bears the burden of success—a Kingdom that runs on the power of the Spirit and not off the turbines of a few highly talented and energetic leaders. I don't have a solution, and it's possible there is not supposed to be a solution as we define it. But I am amazed at the grace that rests upon leaders of spiritual enterprises. I applaud their dedication and smile at their mannerisms.

Small churches have cooks—guys who don paper hats and wrap their lumpy bodies in an apron that used to be white. They have fading tattoos, sweat over the grill and turn out simple fare to customers they know by name. They cater to a crowd of regulars, folks who sit in the same place and order the same thing at the same time every day. These customers no longer need to look at the laminated menus plastered with greasy samples. They're often a family business where the wife runs the register, the son sweeps the floors, and the daughter waits tables. The kids grow up doing their homework in the booth next to the register before they go to Princeton.

Big churches have restaurateurs, guys who wear pressed jackets, trim their nose hairs and sport gold watches that are just the right side of bling. They coach an all-star team of beauty queen waitresses and creative chefs. They hire jazz trios and piano players who sound much too talented for such a gig. They toss their reading glasses on a montage of spread sheets, time cards and quarterly projections that plaster the desk of their offices. They poke their dry eyes and smooth their worry lines in the glow of a green lamp while their family peacefully slumbers above them.

In this current religious economy, pastors sweat in both the kitchen and the board room. Leaders of all sizes and shapes are harried by the insatiable demands of high-maintenance individuals and congregations. Manna-dispensing entrepreneurs log long hours in an unpredictable and often unsafe industry. It should be no surprise that the burn out and blow up rate among pastors has reached a critical state. Statistics about the number of pastors leaving the ministry each month are disconcerting. What is really surprising is that the causality rates are not higher.

Churches are not unique in this respect. Evangelistic organizations spend millions of dollars to execute outreaches that produce nearly negligible results. Even folks who have fled to the presumed safety of home fellowship find themselves working nights and weekends to keep up with the needs of people who look to them for pastoral care. Christian musicians spend their days on the interstate, their evenings in churches and their nights in motels. Seems that, regardless of the task, it takes a lot of energy to keep the customers happy.

THE RIGHT SIZE CHURCH—SUPERSIZING

Recently, there has been an outbreak of opinion-giving about the Church. Everyone it seems has voiced or blogged their opinion about what church is or how church should be done. Ideas about how large a congregation should be or not be seem to lead the discussion. Pundits on both sides of the equation build theological straw men and then burn them at the stake in their new books or latest conferences. I see great things and not so great things in both camps. And because I'm part of that demographic known as everyone, I would like to weigh in with my opinion on the subject.

Large churches can be wonderful expressions of the Kingdom of God. They can do things small congregations simply can't. They can staff Christian schools and take up single offerings that will construct an entire church in a third world country. They can provide livable wages and health insurance benefits to staff and pastors so they don't have to work two jobs to finance the ongoing work of their churches. They attract people who would never visit a small church for fear of being asked too many questions. Like large fishing trawlers, they are able to go further from shore and let down their nets in fisheries the smaller boats simply can't get to.

Large churches are often the inevitable consequence of highly gifted, anointed and faithful individuals who accumulate droves of loyal believers as they faithfully serve the Lord with integrity for many years. Churches often get larger because they provide a high quality of ministry that meets the needs of individuals and families. They grow because they work hard at being relevant and effective in the communities God has strategically located them in. They grow because they are healthy.

Large churches can also be very unhealthy. They tend to attract religious vagabonds who enjoy the anonymity of large gatherings—places where their lifestyle will remain unknown and, therefore, unquestioned by those seated around them. They can foster a patron-centered expression of Christianity that accommodates a culture demanding approbation and accommodation. These are high-maintenance congregations who have been trained to give but not trained to live. They can become congregations comprised of individuals and families whose lifestyles are often blighted by the same immorality that plagues the culture around them. Motivational chats replace Biblical preaching and organizational charts ape the latest corporate model.

Small churches can be wonderful expressions of the Kingdom of God. They can do things large congregations simply can't. They grow in places that are unable to support the needs of their larger peers. They spring up in the nooks and crannies of cultures where it is illegal to meet in large gatherings. They provide a level of community and accountability that is almost impossible to duplicate once a congregation grows past a certain numerical point. They can have picnics and church suppers that everyone can attend. Like small fishing boats with shallow drafts, they are able to access places larger boats simply cannot get to.

Small churches can also be very unhealthy. They can attract religious vagabonds who enjoy exerting a level of influence they would never be able to wield in a larger congregation. Visitors to small churches often feel unwelcome; they sense the dominating personalities of entrenched leadership and the suffocating presence of families who have owned the land for generations. Every head at the manna trough turns as they walk in; every eye looks them up and down before turning back to their blue plate special. The sign out front reads, "All welcome," but the spirit inside says, "Get off my porch or I'll shoot ya!"

Small churches welcome each new pastor with placards and gifts and then run them off with ballot boxes stuffed with the votes of folks who haven't been in church since they voted for Goldwater or Kennedy. During the turf wars, the souls of pastors and their wives get burned up in the fireplace of religious hovels. Those that stay take on the look of the inbred religious community where everyone talks the same, thinks the same and eventually starts even looking the same.

THE TAB

God's people have always pooled their wealth to accomplish things together that they cannot accomplish alone. The escapees of Egypt donated their things to build the tabernacle in the wilderness. The disciples of Jesus carried a common purse so they could cover the expenses for their communal existence. David and Solomon taxed the nation of Israel to build the temple. The apostles received offerings from the early church to finance the ministry that was flowing through them and through the church.

Similarly today, we pool our resources to provide a living wage to those who labor fulltime in Kingdom work. We enable missionaries, pastors, student ministers and other Christian workers to devote their time and energy to the work that God has assigned them to without the draining distraction of secular careers and jobs. We pool our resources to purchase property, to build buildings, to create a brick-and-mortar infrastructure necessary to provide the institutional security to people who have little or no stability in their own homes. The sharing of corporate resources is essential for good stewardship. This is why Paul collected the offering for the relief of the famine in Judea (2 Cor. 9:1ff); it would have been moronic for each believer to book a ticket to Jerusalem and individually drop off his gift.

I'm worried that America's megachurches of today could become tomorrow what the cathedrals of Europe are today—rusting hulks of a bygone age when the construction of edifices became the central purpose of a community. I'm concerned that having the highest steeple in the city has distracted us from the real mission of constructing mature believers. I worry that the building project my home church is about to begin will become an energy draining vortex, pulling us away from the mission of investing in the flesh and blood edifice called Church. This angst causes me to put my tool belt on slowly, look the blueprints over carefully and most importantly follow the Carpenter closely.

All of us should have some concern when a high percentage of our corporate wealth is being funneled into servicing the debt incurred during the construction of buildings and facilities. Big mortgages have the potential to cast long shadows over the Body. The first capital fund drive ends, and another one starts almost immediately. Debt becomes the enemy. Pastors become fundraisers and find themselves detached from the calling that led them into fulltime Christian work. When money dries up, we hire consultants who are skilled in extracting wealth from folks who have already given far and above their tithe. Proven techniques for extracting the wealth hidden deep beneath the congregations surface.

THE SINGLES SCENE

Debt has the potential to unwholesomely influence the way we do ministry. An unseemly temptation not restricted to large churches, all kinds of institutions and ministry organizations large and small can become more interested with the Bride's endowment than her health. I know this will sound crass, but rich girls always look more attractive to potential suitors than poor ones. A lot of money seems to affect ecclesiastical institutions the same way alcohol and poor lighting clouds the vision of nightclub patrons. The little black dress of wealth can mesmerize all of us.

Tipsy pastors and fundraisers stagger about shamelessly, hitting on the members of the Body with the biggest chests of treasure. And lest we get a touch sanctimonious and pretend we are not capable of such indiscretions, we should remember that, after apparently a wee bit too much feasting with the boys, Jacob was shocked to have woken up with Leah. And like the not-so-clever Jacob, we too find ourselves serving an unscrupulous taskmaster for many more years than we ever intended. We are trapped in the land of appeasement and compromise until the hip of our pride and pursuit of success is put out of joint by the renaming power of divine encounter.

Every Christian has the opportunity to imitate the Redeemer whenever we have interaction with His Bride. We have the honor of steering a wide berth around any appearance of favoritism based on property, talent or influence. I've never seen a trustee's or deacon's office auctioned off on E-bay. Yet, it would be refreshingly honest if some institution actually had the courage to openly do that which has been done not so clandestinely all along. Unfortunately, it seems like decisions are still carefully stirred and not shaken;

visions are elegantly garnished to impress and tantalize the fickle sensibilities of skittish vixens who threaten to run off if they encounter something their spoiled taste buds finds unpleasing.

It's not just the suitors who can find themselves compromised in these situations. Well-endowed patrons become intoxicated by the potent cocktail of influence. Pretty girls quickly learn how to simultaneously flirt with competing ministerial and institutional suitors. They bask in the flattery, purr under the soft strokes to their egos and revel in the shameless efforts to win their affections. All that attention fertilizes a growing sense of entitlement that shades them from the healthy light of honest conversation and Biblical correction.

I don't want to belabor this point, yet it bears repeating that this temptation to practice favoritism is very powerful for those in positional leadership. I must confess that I have succumbed to this temptation more than once and must remain vigilant not to fall into this sin again. While I have never assigned seating to rich or poor in the congregation as James wrote about, I have on several occasions spent inordinate amounts of time and energy attempting to recruit or retain those members of His Bride who gave lots of money, had special gifting or wielded large amounts of influence in the congregation. It is why savvy church shoppers and hoppers are very careful not to put their contact information on visitor cards lest they be inundated with the inevitable outpouring of letters, e-mails, cards and follow-up phone calls from guys they met on Sunday morning.

I trust the motivation of the majority of these overtures is completely noble, that the welfare of the Bride is foremost in the hearts and minds of these suitors. But, unfortunately, it seems that blind pursuit of numerical growth and financial stability continues to impair the judgment of many leaders. This blind pursuit has intoxicated a generation of church-goers with the liqueurs of entitlement that make it impossible for them to walk a straight line.

In a culture overrun with choices on every level, fussy religious consumers can avail themselves to almost any nuance of doctrine or distinctive. And while the temptation to pander to these ever-changing expectations is profound, we would do well to keep our eyes and hearts focused on the face of the Bride and know her Father is watching and her Fiancé is about to show up.

I'm not sure that exploring this restaurant-church metaphor has gotten us any closer to discovering the free lunch foreshadowed by Ruth. However, I trust that this critique of modern church life will steer us away from some of the pitfalls that trapped our friends in the past and that our corporate ambition in this age will be kindled to rediscover the ancient place, the eternal place where lunch really is free.

CHAPTER 16
Sex

"Remain this night . . . .' So she lay at his feet until morning" (RUTH 3:13).

*"'May you be blessed of the Lord, my daughter.
You have shown your last kindness to be better than the first by
not going after young men, whether poor or rich'"* (RUTH 3:10).

*"'. . . may your house be like the house of Perez
who Tamar bore to Judah . . .'"* (RUTH 4:12).

D id you skip all the other chapters in this book and read this one first? Now be honest; no one else will know you did. Okay, maybe you're one of the few who didn't, but lots of people skip ahead to chapters about sex before they read the rest of the book they are browsing through.

Don't be embarrassed if you did; both men and women, young and old alike, are interested in sex, especially Christians I might add. But if I'm going to be honest as well, I must tell you that this chapter is not just about having sex; it's also about *not* having sex. But go ahead and read this chapter first anyway because it helps explain in part why we want to spend the night with someone, why we don't want to be alone. It explores the prophetic template of romance and marriage that our Redeemer wants us to experience with Him, and it explains a little, I hope, of why we don't want to sleep alone and why the Redeemer wants us to spend the night with Him.

NUCLEAR SEX

Bringing two people together is like having radioactive fuel and neutrons in close proximity. A reaction occurs that produces a fantastic amount of heat. When properly regulated and contained, nuclear energy is a clean and safe alternative to burning fossil fuels. Unregulated nuclear reactions wipe entire cities off the map, or create a mass so hot that it melts through the earth's mantle. Uncontained meltdowns spread deadly radioactivity into the air that contaminates the environment and makes everyone who is exposed to it sick. Likewise, unregulated and uncontained sexuality spreads destruction everywhere it goes. Nuclear families are split apart; disease and cancers manifest in those contaminated by its lethal radioactivity.

Marriage is God's gift to humanity. Holy matrimony regulates and contains His gift of sexuality. We are sexual beings by design, and God loves every aspect of His creation. He hardwired sexuality into our collective soul to both fulfill us and lead His wayward creation back to Himself. Go anywhere in the world, and you'll find that people pair off and make babies. Marriage, which can only be defined as heterosexual monogamy, has the greatest potential for meeting the God-given need for companionship, sexual fulfillment and reproduction. Humanity is drawn toward exclusive relationships because we are created in His image and likeness—an image and likeness that demand exclusivity.

During the "sexual revolution" of the 1960's, a well-known anthropologist cited "evidence" that there were pristine cultures able to enjoy "free sex" without the limitations of heterosexual monogamy. She claimed there was anthropological evidence to verify the arguments of those championed by the proponents' sexual promiscuity. Not until later did this so-called evidence come under careful scientific scrutiny. When it was, it was discovered to have been false. Human beings do not typically share their sexual partners and are not inclined to raise the offspring of others as their own. God is monogamous, and so the humanity that He's created in His image and likeness is also predisposed to seek out monogamy to alleviate loneliness.

Ruth and Boaz did not have sex until after they were married. Their sexuality found expression in the God-given safety of marriage. I'm aware that well-meaning Bible scholars and some Hebrew language experts have tried to explain that this phrase "laying at the feet" was a euphemism for a sexual encounter—that the pagan practices of the Canaanite's culture included sexual relations that took place during the agricultural cycles of sowing, reaping and threshing of grain. However, we can be quite certain Boaz and Ruth did not have sex the night she lay at his feet. We can be confident because the Bible would have told us if they did. God is honest, and it follows that His Scriptures are honest. He doesn't inspire double entendre and wink at indiscretions when telling the stories about the lives of His people.

The Scriptures are not bashful in telling us about the sexuality, or even the sexual failures, of its characters. These unedited biographies have given real hope and great grace to their readers in all generations. We have more than enough information about David watching Bathsheba taking a bath and Abraham doing it with Hagar. We can even be tempted to blush when we read Solomon's graphic descriptions of his voluptuous wife. The Bible gives us the account of *coitus interruptus* being used as birth control, and we know that Noah got drunk and took off all his clothes. The Bible's verbal camera was not controlled by the censors that policed the Hollywood movies in bygone generations. Its verbal images do not fade into innocuous landscapes or pan away when lovers make love or sexually sin on its historic screen. If Boaz and Ruth had sex before they were married, we would have known about it.

Of course, no marriage or relationship, for that matter, will ever completely succeed in meeting all our needs or desires. Life is full of problems, many of which can interfere with the enjoyment of normal human relationship. Sin separates us from God and one another. This realization, the discovery that even the most intimate of human relationships cannot fulfill our deepest needs, is crucial. Becoming disillusioned with human institutions and relationships is a painful and necessary step in a wholehearted pursuit of God. Until we have exhausted our hopes and fantasies that another person can make us happy, we will waste our lives in either a futile attempt to find the perfect spouse, or even worse, the idolatry of attempting to mold our existing spouses into the perfect mate.

FANTASY ISLAND

Humans are castaways. Each of us is trapped on the desert island of our individuality. Our connectedness with others, no matter how strong or intense, does not alter this reality. We are born into perpetual solitary confinement, a flesh and blood island from which only death will release us. It is a difficult truth to accept and one which we usually try to forget. We entwine our thoughts and our bodies with others to soothe the pain of our isolation. Like Boaz, we ask others to remain the night.

When we first become aware of our aloneness, we do everything we can to be rescued from it. The onset of puberty heightens our awareness of being alone. God-given hormones intoxicate us and awaken feelings and passions that will influence us for the rest of our natural lives. Girls giggle about boys; boys continually think about sex. We date, we kiss, and we masturbate. We frantically run laps around our tiny island, looking for the rescue ship. We kindle huge bonfires on the beach and hope someone will notice us, and we spell out S-O-S in the sands of the internet.

We lash the logs of our souls into flimsy rafts and set ourselves adrift in the tide. We scan the empty horizon, day after day. We stare into the empty sea of humanity, hoping, praying and wishing with all our might that a ship will appear—that true love will sail into our horizon. Imagination turns driftwood into boats and clouds into sails. The sun parches us, and we drink the salt water of perversion and immorality that further inflames our thirst for fresh intimacy. The sea grows angry in the night; the waves and squalls tear apart our rafts. We awaken with our faces in the sand, waves lapping at our legs, and we get on our knees and realize we're back on the same old island.

I'm so glad I'm married; I can't image life without my wife. At low tide, it's almost as if our islands are connected; we think the same thoughts, feel the same feelings and say the same things at the same time. I like to tell folks that when I married my wife I hit the lottery. I suppose by human standards we have a great marriage. Yet, it's with a measure of irony we both agree that the key to our marital bliss is that we don't expect each other to take away all our loneliness. We are not truly focused on our marriage or family; we try to focus on God. It is His presence that tempers our expectations.

Maybe you're at a place of discouragement or disillusionment right now. Perhaps a series of unfulfilling experiences and relationships have dashed your hopes and left you feeling more alone than ever. This can be a good place; it is actually a place of emotional wholeness when we accept the spiritual and emotional realities of living in a fallen world where creation is subjected to futility—where we come to understand that loneliness is an integral part of the human condition and accept that even the most intimate of all human relationships, no matter how ideal, will never completely cure our lonely condition.

So it's a good day when we let the fires go out and let the tide wash away our advertisements. We stop looking at the horizon; we stop trying to escape our solitary existence on the island of our souls. We stop expecting others to take away our loneliness and accept our situation. Until we accept our confinement, our lives are fraught with emotional highs and lows fed by the adrenaline of a new relationship or novel encounters. Until we accept our confinement, we damage our existing relationships with expectation or, even worse, insistence, that our husbands or wives can, and therefore must, meet all our needs. It's a good day when we call off the man or woman hunt and start searching for the only One who will satisfy our deepest needs.

Yet in spite of our best efforts to let God alone meet our needs, we and all of humanity are continually and intuitively drawn to the God-given pattern for exclusive sexual relationships. This drawing seems even more intense for believers, and it may explain why you're reading this chapter first. When the Spirit of God enters the human soul, He kindles an obsessive passion for intimacy. The Spirit cries out for intimacy with God. Our souls crave intimacy with our families and long for intimacy with His people. God created marriage as the ultimate human relationship and therefore is the best metaphor for salvation and relationship with Him. Marriage captures and embodies the passion and love God has for humanity.

As a side bar to this prophetic template of the Bride at the Redeemer's feet, Boaz's and Ruth's abstinence until marriage is an excellent example of sexual purity for any couple. Two things, of course, stand out in this account. First, we can abstain from sexual sin even in situations when the temptation is great and no one else would know about it. Second, the engagement was short. For serious-minded Christians who value their purity, as I've said before, these are good lessons.

It's my conviction that Christian spirituality should be as intense and enjoyable as holy expressions of our sexuality. The enemy has wanted us to embrace a prudish, Victorian-era kind of spirituality—non-orgasmic worship and prayer experience that is perfunctory, but not really passionate, where we spiritually leave our clothes on. The Spirit of God is leading the Bride of Christ into a place of intimacy that is so satisfying, so enjoyable that the pleasures of sin pale in comparison—a place of intimacy that produces babies and releases the wholesale affections and resources of the Redeemer.

BABES IN DIAPERLAND

How is it that girls who stop traffic marry men who wear diapers? We've all seen the checkout line tabloids that seem to be continually running headlines about these unusual couples. Apparently, the titillating details of union between 80-something-year-old men and 20-something-year-old women sells papers. Forgive my cynicism, but it must be noted that these grandfather-aged grooms have only one common attribute that makes them so irresistible to these glamorous beauties. Money, and lots of it, is the ultimate love potion. Never mind grinding up the horns of a nearly extinct Rhinoceros or getting the local witch doctor to utter mumbo-jumbo while killing a chicken in front of that special someone's picture. Just get yourself a few hundred million bucks, have your lawyer change the will, and *"Shazam"* Prom queens and NFL cheerleaders are lining up to share your bed and wipe lunch off your chin.

Was Ruth a gold digger? Was she the archetype of these de-facto prostitutes who are willing to trade their affections for wealth? At first glance, it certainly seems possible. Honest inquiry demands that we objectively examine the evidence we do have and accept the facts as they are. No point in trying to kick sand over the messy and embarrassing histories of God's people. If Ruth is to serve as a powerful prophetic image of the Bride of Christ in our age, we must be willing to look the historical record of Scripture squarely in the face and then draw our conclusions and make our applications.

We know for certain there was a significant age difference between Boaz and Ruth. We don't know exactly how many years separated these two, but the disparity was enough that her age is referenced twice in this short book. Often the Scriptures record the ages of our spiritual ancestors at key moments in their lives, but not in this case. We are certain of this age disparity because both Boaz and the elders of Bethlehem state what must have been obvious to anyone who knew these two. Specifically, that Ruth was both young and attractive and Boaz was quite a bit older.

The prophetic insight for the Bride of Christ living in the last days is the amazing attraction the Ageless One has to young people. One of the most amazing phenomenons of Kingdom life is the abundance of young people who are committed to a deep and abiding monogamous relationship with Christ. Devoted young people, who are only a mouse click or text message away from relationships with youthful suitors, choose to embrace the person of Christ and the eternal values of the Father. Like Ruth they could *"go after young men,"* but they choose to lay at the feet of the Redeemer. Youth are the lifeblood of any Christian movement; the Redeemer is especially endeared to those who spend their youth pursuing Him. How we choose to spend the precious and few years of our youth is often a down payment on a lifelong commitment to Him.

A second and possibly even more powerful prophetic application is the age of Boaz when he married Ruth. Like Abraham and Jacob before him, he fathers a son at an age when most folks are done having children. Today, there are countless opportunities for the mature members of Christ to enter into reproductive relationships that will bless future generations. Boaz provides a prophetic template for older saints to embrace unions with more youthful members of the Body.

A closer examination of the blessing pronounced by the elders of Bethlehem over the union of Boaz and Ruth will provide comfort and hope to all of us who have a less-than-perfect sexual history. Our Father's selection of people who have non-typical family stories is nothing new. Ruth's marriage to a wealthy older man is trivial when compared to the examples that the elders choose to reference in their blessings. If you have ever thought that you or someone else's life history disqualified you or him from being part of God's Kingdom, please acquaint yourself with the following stories before you pass such judgment on yourself or others.

THE TOAST

The city elders' blessing of the marriage of Boaz to Ruth is the most perplexing part of the entire book of Ruth. At first glance, to someone not familiar with the biographies of the patriarchs, it seems innocuous enough—some-

thing akin to the best man's toast at a wedding reception. We've all pretend-
ed to listen to these generic well-wishes for a long and happy life, blah blah
blah, now let's cut the cake. However, the elders of Bethlehem actually bless
the union of Boaz and Ruth by citing both a polygamous marriage and a tryst
with a supposed prostitute. These two complicated relationships are invoked
by the elders of Bethlehem as the blessing of Boaz's union with his new bride.

First, they reference Jacob and his sister wives: Leah and Rachel. Jacob,
the patriarch of Israel, married Leah and Rachel when he was 83 years old.
He was tricked into marriage with the older sister Leah by his conniving
father-in-law, Laban, who was desperate to retain his gratis services. Jacob had
brought financial prosperity to his uncle Laban during the seven years he
worked for the privilege of marrying Leah's younger sister Rachel. After seven
years of indentured servitude, he goes to the wedding feast and wakes up the
next morning with Rachel's older sister Leah—an excellent example I might
add of why we should not drink too much at weddings. Laban's machinations
coerced Jacob into another seven years of service in exchange for getting to
marry Rachel the next week. I've always wondered what sisters would talk
about if they were married to the same guy; the weather I guess.

While polygamy tests my toleration, what rankles me even more is that
Jacob was 83 when he got married twice in eight days. My eyes bulge at the
thought of an 83-year-old man entering a polygamous marriage with two
young sisters and fathering twelve children in a ten year period. In an age long
before pharmacological assistance, the reproductive exploits of a man who
today would be under the care of a gerontologist is the stuff of legends.
Geriatric sexual icons like Hugh Heffner look like amateurs in the presence
of Jacob. While we might not be comfortable with this reality, the fact is that
Jacob was a very sexually active senior citizen when he fathered the patriarchs.
The elders of Bethlehem are blessing Boaz with heir-producing virility in his
advanced years. It's a great blessing!

The second Biblical couple invoked at the blessing of Boaz's union with
Ruth is the union between Judah and Tamar. This citation is much more dis-
turbing than the first because their son, Perez, was conceived via an illicit one-
time encounter between these two related and unmarried persons. The titil-

lating account is detailed in Genesis 38, and it reads more like the cover of a tawdry romantic novel than the history of God's chosen people. Here is a thumbnail description of the relationship.

Tamar was married to Er, Judah's oldest son. After God put Er to death, his younger brother Onan was obliged to father a child for his brother according to traditions of the day. Eventually, this obligation to father children on behalf of one's deceased brother was codified in Mosaic Law (Deut. 25:5ff). Onan, however, was unwilling to impregnate his sister-in-law. The details of his sexual encounter could have only been known to Tamar. The infamous *"spilling his seed on the ground"* leaves Tamar childless and widowed again because Onan's selfish refusal to give his brother an heir was quickly punished, and he was struck dead by God like his brother before him.

Judah is now bereft of both sons who were married to Tamar. In spite of his evident mistrust and suspicion of Tamar, he promises to give his youngest son, Shelah, to her when he becomes of marrying age. It's very possible that Judah believed Tamar to be somehow culpable in the death of his two boys. Like most parents, he would have found it difficult to believe that his sons were evil and doubted Tamar's accusation that Onan had done such a thing. Undoubtedly, he hoped that a girl like he believed Tamar to be would not live a chaste life during the years it took his youngest son to reach a proper age for marriage. His instant condemnation of Tamar, when she is found to be pregnant, to the flames reserved for adulteresses reveal both his suspicions and his flagrant hypocrisy.

Of course, Tamar was not the kind of girl her father-in-law believed her to be. In fact, she lived as a chaste widow in her father's house and patiently waited until Shelah came of age. Judah, on the other hand, feared that Tamar was some sort of *black widow* and continued to delay giving his son to her. After a season, she realized Judah had no intention of ever allowing his son to consummate their marriage. Like all women of her culture, she would have been virtually powerless to pressure her father-in-law into fulfilling his promise. So she concocts a Labanesque-like plan to entangle her father-in-law in a web of intrigue from which there would be no escape.

In a ruse that would have made her ancestor, Laban, stand up and applaud, Tamar actually managed to get Judah to unknowingly impregnate her after his persistent reneging on his promise. In the end, her father-in-law apologized, she was vindicated, and she got twin male heirs to raise. She accomplished all this by disguising herself as a cult prostitute and successfully enticing her father-in-law to have anonymous sex with her. She sprung her trap while he was away from home, traveling on a sheep-shearing business trip with his friend. (Extra-Biblical records state that Judah claims to have been drunk at the time, another reason not to drink too much when you're at a sheep-shearing convention.)

The Bible tells us that, in lieu of immediate payment for services rendered, she negotiated to retain several of Judah's personal possessions, including his signet ring and staff. Three months later, she displayed these objects as irrefutable evidence of her father's-in-law out of town dalliance. I guess what happened in Timnah didn't stay in Timnah any better than what happens in Las Vegas stays in Las Vegas today. Staffs and credit card numbers, seals and venereal diseases have a way of finding their way back home.

So what is the blessing in all this? What were the elders of the city thinking when they uttered this invocation? I believe they were reminding everyone that God has a way of redeeming even the most complicated personal situations. It's more than likely that they did not quite understand why the most eligible guy in the city would want to marry a young foreigner. Yet, they profoundly understood that God's family tree was full of kids like Perez, children who were innocently born outside of the protective and ideal environment of marriage. It would be good for all of us to hear and receive this blessing spoken over every child, even the ones with less-than-perfect parents.

CHAPTER 17
The Girl not the Gold

"Then Boaz said, 'On the day you buy the field from the hand of Naomi, you must also acquire Ruth the Moabitess'" (RUTH 4:5).

T en days after graduating high school, a friend and I drove into Canada. Polite border agents smiled and waved us over the border from northern New York into the province of Quebec. We were amateur hippies, two suburban kids cruising around wasting time and getting wasted.

We camped in deserted gravel pits, swam in icy water and gave rides to hitch-hikers at every opportunity. Our only real objective was to make sure my buddy got to Michigan the following week to meet up with his parents on the campus of the university he was planning to attend in the fall. So we meandered through northern Quebec and Ontario for a week, eventually turning south to cross back into the States via the Upper Peninsula of Michigan. Somewhere near the border, we picked up a Canadian kid who said he had never been in the States, so we invited him to ride with us for his first visit to our country.

Crossing into Canada had been a breeze, so we naïvely thought that getting back into America would be little more than a formality. Nearing the border, we merged into the single-file line of cars and kept our music blaring all the way up to the customs booth. Pulling us over was a no brainer. After all, we were three motley-looking, red-eyed kids listening to Pink Floyd in a VW.

The officer asked if we were American citizens, and we said we were, but the kid in the back told him he was a Canadian citizen whom we had picked up hitchhiking. We flashed disbelieving and sarcastic smiles at each other when he pointed us to a parking area off to the side where other officers stood waiting to receive us. A small knot formed in my stomach.

They guided us into the parking area with hand motions that looked like they belonged on the deck of an aircraft carrier. I turned off the engine, but they took my keys, and I stopped smirking as the officer escorted us toward the U.S. customs offices.

As we entered the building, I glanced back just in time to see a couple of other border guards with mirrors and flashlights as they began to rip into the contents of the vehicle. The knot that was looped in my stomach when we were asked to pull over was pulled tight when the doors we entered locked behind us. My friend and I were separated, taken to different holding rooms where we would have to wait until they completed the examination of my car.

After only a couple of minutes, one of the agents searching my car came in. He was carrying some of the things we had casually thrown under the seats while waiting in the line of cars, hoping to cross the border. The things were placed on the table in front of me, and the officer asked me if any of the things belonged to me.

"Well, ah, you see, ah . . . I guess that Canadian kid must have put that stuff in my car. You know those Canadians . . ."

The demeanor of the officer questioning me turned surprisingly friendly and almost conciliatory. He saw my growing fear and assured me that if we cooperated everything would be okay. He said that I would have to be searched because they had discovered these illegal things in my car. He informed me that, regardless of whose stuff it was, I was responsible for anything found in my vehicle. I was told to place the contents of my pockets on the table. Pocket knife, matches, Export A's, fishing weights, colorful Canadian money—everything but a frog was dumped from my jeans and sweater. Next, I was told to place my hands on the table. I was thoroughly patted down to make sure I had completely emptied my pockets. I hadn't. The customs agent pulled something from my sweater's pocket I had not so cleverly concealed there. He grinned and threw it on the table. Like taking candy from a baby, I suppose.

Then he told me to pull down my pants. "What?" I asked, thinking surely I must have misunderstood him.

"Pull down your pants," he said, just as clearly as he said it the first time.

The knot in my stomach was synched another notch. My mouth fell open, my eyes rolled, and I obeyed.

Later, we were given a ride to a police station where we were fined and scolded by the local chief of police. They drove us back to the border where we paid another fee to retrieve my impounded VW. We nervously drove away, thankful that we had not been trying to get into Turkey, and in the end, it turned out to be no big deal. In fact, because we were able to pay the fines and fees immediately, there was no permanent record made of our arrest and detention. We kept some paperwork and receipts as souvenirs of our little adventure. Years later, my friend's mom found his paperwork stashed in their attic. She called my mom, and my mom called me. (I think the government should hire moms to screen people at airports; no one would ever sneak anything past them.)

I share this story because it's my first and only experience with being arrested and the only time I've ever been searched. The experience revealed to me something about how I have approached God, how I have often misinterpreted the events and circumstances of my life. Somehow, I mistakenly construed entering the Kingdom of God to be something akin to trying to enter the U.S. But, of course, it's not a completely accurate way of understanding entering the Kingdom of God because God's primary interests are not confiscating my contraband, fining or scolding me. His primary interest is me.

Boaz's redemption of Ruth is a prophetic picture of Christ's redemption of humanity. The incarnation, death and resurrection of Christ accomplished the redemption of human souls, not our possessions. Boaz's desire to redeem Ruth was not about the acquisition of more farmland. His desire to redeem Ruth was fueled by the intense love in his heart for the young woman and not the property she was attached to. The speed with which he pursues redemption was fueled by the passion that her vulnerability had stirred in him the night before. The romantic bond between Ruth and Boaz is a prophetic picture of God's intense desire for us. Redemption is not God's method of gaining control of our stuff; redemption is God's way of gaining control of us. The Redeemer is after His Bride.

THE BORDER

It's a mistake to be as naïve as my friend and I were when we tried to cross the border with all our junk. Likewise, it's a mistake to think we can enter the

Kingdom of God with all the baggage and illicit material we have been collecting over the years. His Kingdom cannot be entered when we are conceal-
ing anything from Him. In this respect, coming into the Kingdom is like
crossing the border except, of course, nothing can ever be successfully smuggled passed the Omniscient Inspector.

Nonetheless, we show up at the border of His domain with lots of
garbage stuffed in our pockets and hidden under our seats. He smiles and asks
us to put it all on the table. No doubt, this search of our being by the Holy
Spirit is a very real and necessary step in lightening our load so we can fully
enter into the fullness of what He wants for us. The theological term for this
ongoing process of inspection and confiscation is called sanctification, a necessary component of every Christian's journey. *"Pursue peace with all men, and
the sanctification without which no one will see the Lord"* (Heb. 12:14). He con-
fiscates our things so we won't be distracted or defiled by them.

But unlike the involuntary search at the border, the Lord simply asks us
what we have on us. If we try to hide things from His search, sooner or later,
convictions or circumstances coerce us into emptying our own pockets, the
putting on the table of the habits and secret sins that plague our souls. This
quasi-voluntary process of sanctification is His chosen method of removing
from us anything that is dangerous and toxic to our souls and the health of
our fellow citizens. The term *quasi-voluntary* seems most appropriate. I don't
view sanctification as completely voluntary. For me, it is only when He brings
some level of discomfort to my existence that I start to discard the trash I've
been collecting. Occasionally, I've even been foolish enough to think, because
He didn't say something to me or take something from me immediately by
force, that He approved of whatever it was I had on me.

Yet the real dissimilarity between my experience at the border and my
ongoing journey further into the Kingdom is what happens after the contraband and illegal substances have been confiscated. For my friend and me, we
just paid the fines and drove off; there's not even a record of the arrest on file
as far as I know. This is how I saw repentance and forgiveness. I would get
caught, apologize, pay the fine of emotional penance and then go about my
business. Of course, there would be no record of my sin, no remembrance of

my iniquity. I am still happy to quote Psalm 103:12, *"As far as the east is from the west, so far has He removed our transgressions from us."* This is all very Biblical, very true and essential for any Christian's progress in the faith.

Getting caught doing something wrong was so traumatic that I would do just about anything to get out of the detention area as quickly as possible. Afterwards, I could sit in church and listen to a pure hellfire and brimstone repentance sermon and feel pretty confident that I had already turned all my pockets inside out and dumped everything on the altar. My Christian faith was becoming increasingly defined by what I didn't do. I began to mistakenly appraise the authenticity of other people's faith by what they didn't do, too. "Don't smoke, don't chew, and don't go with girls who do." I hate to admit it, but this little puritanical jingle pretty well described my narrow understanding of redemption. Secular music, wine, dancing at weddings, Christmas trees and refined sugar were all on my blacklist at one time or another.

An incident occurred a few months after we were married that sums up my understanding of the Kingdom at that time. We had just purchased an old red Toyota station wagon so Neen would not be stranded out in the country when I was at work or church. The first time I drove the car, I programmed the tuner to the Christian radio station, which I might add, had not changed its programming in 20 years. A few weeks later, I had occasion to drive the car again and was perplexed to find the radio tuned to an adult contemporary station, so I tuned it back to the Gospel station and went about my business.

A few weeks later, I drove the car again and discovered the same secular station was tuned into the radio. Instead of driving off, I got out of the car and marched into the house to ask my bride if she knew anything about this radio business. How offended, shocked and disappointed I was when the woman I thought was truly holy confessed that she listened to secular music. What had me confused is that I also knew my wife to be one of the purest people I have ever known. What had me confused was how she could listen to that kind of music and still be holier than I. What I failed to understand was that He was not just after her stuff, my stuff or anyone else's stuff—that separating our bodies, souls and spirits from stuff was just the beginning of our journey into His Kingdom.

PAST THE BORDER

I have been to Poland. During a flight over Europe, our plane was grounded in Warsaw because heavy fog had made it impossible to land in Kiev, Ukraine, where we were scheduled to land. For three or four hours, we milled about the airport in Poland until the fog burned off in Kiev and we could resume our journey. We were never allowed out of the airport because we didn't have visas, and we were restricted to a small section of the terminal to wait. So technically I've been to Poland, but I have only seen a few glimpses of the land through the windows of the airport. Like the hitchhiker we picked up, he too officially made it into America, but he never made it past the border. But there is so much more to discover about a land than what can be seen at an airport or customs house.

As long as I viewed the Kingdom of God as a place where God was simply trying to separate me from my stuff, I remained confined to that tiny corner of the Kingdom where the confiscation of contraband was the main activity—a myopic ghetto where everyone was under suspicion, where self-appointed bloodhounds read books on how to sniff out doctrines and practices that were being smuggled in and corrupting the Church.

I had souvenirs from the gift shop to commemorate the visit—baptismal certificates, church membership cards and a shellacked piece of wood with something about footprints. These were mementos of a visit, but no evidence of the exploration of the expansive, dynamic, history-changing, supernatural Kingdom that He was inviting me to be part of. Maybe I should get a T-shirt that says, "I got saved, but all I got was this dumb T-shirt saying I got saved."

It took years for all of me to get more than a few yards over the border, to really believe that the purpose of redemption was to make me part of His Body and Bride. For as long as my focus was on not doing wrong things, the temptation to do wrong things became the center of my Christian life. As soon as I would master one habit or escape the power of a particular sin, another vice would jump up and demand my attention. Unfortunately, the issues that were taking my energies and attention became smaller and smaller. It wasn't enough to be free from the immoral behaviors clearly prohibited by God. I had become the white-gloved inspector, the religious zealot looking for the slightest evidence of dust in my life and even in the lives of others. The Way was narrow I affirmed and was getting narrower by the minute.

I am so grateful that my *sinless* streaks were not as impressive to Him as they were to me, so grateful that my inevitable strikeouts neither discouraged nor dissuaded Him from the relentless pursuit of my total devotion and affection. In His mercy, I have come to see that my commuting to and fro across the border and getting my stuff confiscated were just a prelude to His plan to fully naturalize me into a fulltime citizen of His Nation. His Redemption of my soul and His love for who I am, and not what I possess, are what makes Him different than my retarded understanding of the Kingdom as only a few sterilized rooms near the border.

THE GIRL NOT THE GROUND

Remember that Boaz was not the closest redeemer. This other fellow was first in line and was apparently very interested in acquiring the property that Naomi had up for redemption. Boaz had already warned Ruth in the night that someone else was first in line and also may have suspected that the other guy was going to want this piece of property. I'm sure in those sleepless hours with Ruth at his feet he tumbled the predicament over and over in his mind. Then his love conceived a plan, a way to negotiate the redemption whereby a property-hungry redeemer would be differentiated from a love-hungry redeemer. It would be a risky strategy; he could lose Ruth if the plan failed. His redemption would be done legally, but it would also need to be done in such a way that the other relative would be glad to forfeit his right to the land because of the price of redemption also involved acquiring a girl.

In the morning as Ruth slipped back home, Boaz went into the town of Bethlehem to set his plan in motion. He went to the city gates, sat down and patiently waited. The city gates were the location where official business like this was conducted. At some point, the other guy passed by. Boaz called him over and had him sit down. He gathered the necessary quorum of ten elders required to transact official business and began the negotiation.

Boaz was working the deal very coolly. He was obviously on good terms with both his kinsman and the elders but was not about to tell them that he was madly in love with the girl from Moab. From their vantage point, he was just trying to expedite the redemption of some family farmland, a business deal, plain and simple. Note his low-key statement: *"So I thought to inform you"* (Ruth 4:4). What a guy, taking his time to let the other potential redeemer know about the great deal on some fine farmland!

You can almost hear him calmly talking about the rich soil, good well, nice view and all the other amenities this piece of property came with. Everyone was probably thinking that Boaz was simply trying to make sure that not only would the property get sold quickly, but that Naomi would get top dollar for her land. Sure enough, the kinsman wanted to redeem the land and was ready to do the deal. He said, *"I will redeem it"* (Ruth 4:4). Some discussion would have ensued about the appropriate purchase price in relationship to the year of Jubilee when all land would be automatically returned to the family (Lev. 25:8). The deal was just about concluded when Boaz lowered the boom.

He said, almost like it was just an afterthought, oh, by the way, *"on the day you buy the field from the hand of Naomi, you must also acquire Ruth the Moabitess, the widow of the deceased, in order to raise up the name of the deceased on his inheritance"* (Ruth 4:5). This was the coup de grace, the death blow that separated the guy who wanted the land from the guy who wanted the girl. I imagine Boaz looking him in the eye while the poor guy pondered this last-minute revelation. He must have taken a moment to think about how he was going to explain this latest purchase to his wife. The scene flashes through his mind.

Kinsman: Hi, honey. I'm home. Brought you some flowers and a nice cut of lamb for the grill tonight.

Wife: (She comes out of the kitchen wiping hands on a dish towel.) Oh, how nice. I'll put them in a vase . . . what's the occasion?

Kinsman: Well, you know that piece of land that belonged to Elimelech?

Wife: The one by the road they used to grow barley on?

Kinsman: Yeah, that's the one. Well, I bought it today. And don't worry about the price. I figure it will pay for itself in just three seasons; I made a real deal on it.

Wife: That is wonderful; you're so smart with business all the time. (She goes over and kisses her husband and lovingly throws her arms around him. Looking out the window with her chin on his neck, she notices someone standing in the driveway.)

Wife: Honey, there is an attractive young woman standing in the driveway.

Kinsman: Oh, yeah . . . her. I guess I forgot to mention that she was part of the deal. Apparently, she was married to Naomi's youngest son.

Wife: So she will be our servant or something?

Kinsman: Well not exactly. I just need to get her pregnant that's all . . .

Wife: (Interrupts him.) WHAT?!

Kinsman: I knew you would understand. Could you be a doll and sleep on the couch for a couple of weeks?

Of course, we don't know all that this fellow was thinking, but we do know what he said, *"I cannot redeem it for myself, lest I jeopardize my own inheritance. Redeem it for yourself, you may have my right of redemption, for I cannot redeem it"* (Ruth 4:6). The wannabe redeemer flinched; sticker shock set in. Turned out the fine print in the deal included a little Moabite widow who needed to have a baby. So he backed out, passed the sandal, folded his hand and walked out of the showroom and off the pages of Scripture.

We can only imagine the goose flesh that bumped up and down Boaz's skin as he was trying to keep his proper demeanor in front of the elders while the details of the deal were being solemnized. I envision him trying to act all cool and calm. I hear him using his best professional business voice while he says, *"You are witnesses today that I have bought . . . moreover I have acquired Ruth the Moabitess . . . ."* (Ruth 4:9-10).

As the official business wraps up, he perfunctorily shakes a few hands and nods his seen-it-all smile. Meanwhile, there is something completely different happening inside of Boaz. Every fiber of his being has poured onto the streets of his soul to party. A raucous and riotous celebration has spontaneously erupted to commemorate the end of singleness. Happy mobs are dancing in the streets singing, "Here comes the bride." They are climbing light poles, waving flags and kissing strangers while church bells peal. I'm not sure how far it was from the city gates to Naomi's place. But there is one thing I'm pretty sure of, Boaz covered that ground in record time. He got the girl!

NOTES

1. "Absinthe." *Wikipedia, The Free Encyclopedia.* 24 Sep 2009, 20:08 UTC. 24 Sep 2009 <en.wikipedia.org/w/index.php?title=Absinthe&oldid=315983942>.

2. Facts were obtained from the "Absinthe" Wikipedia entry of note 1 above.

3. Facts were obtained from *the Instituto Clomodiro Picado*'s Web site— <www.icp.ucr.ac.cr/index.php>. This site lists the variety of snakes in Costa Rica, the history of Clomodiro Picado, and other information about anti-venin.

4. Opie, Iona and Peter. *The Oxford Dictionary of Nursery Rhymes* (Oxford, England: Oxford University Press, 1997) 66-67.

5. The article from the World Health Organization regarding depression may be found at <news.bbc.co.uk/2/hi/health/6981678.stm>.

Breinigsville, PA USA
10 January 2010
230475BV00003B/8/P